# Accounting Ledger Book

| Name: | Position: |
|---|---|
| Adress: | |
| | |
| Mobile: | |
| Telephone: | |
| Email: | |
| Fax: | |
| | |
| | |

## Book info :

| Book No.: | Continued from book No.: |
|---|---|
| Start Date: | End Date: |

## Notes:

_____

_____

_____

_____

_____

_____

# ACCOUNTING LEDGER

**PAGE.No.**

**Account Name And Number :**

**Year : _____**                    **Month : _____**

| No. | Date | Description | Account | Reference | Debit | − | Credit | + | Total |
|-----|------|-------------|---------|-----------|-------|---|--------|---|-------|
|     |      |             |         |           |       |   |        |   |       |
|     |      |             |         |           |       |   |        |   |       |
|     |      |             |         |           |       |   |        |   |       |
|     |      |             |         |           |       |   |        |   |       |
|     |      |             |         |           |       |   |        |   |       |
|     |      |             |         |           |       |   |        |   |       |
|     |      |             |         |           |       |   |        |   |       |
|     |      |             |         |           |       |   |        |   |       |
|     |      |             |         |           |       |   |        |   |       |
|     |      |             |         |           |       |   |        |   |       |
|     |      |             |         |           |       |   |        |   |       |
|     |      |             |         |           |       |   |        |   |       |
|     |      |             |         |           |       |   |        |   |       |
|     |      |             |         |           |       |   |        |   |       |
|     |      |             |         |           |       |   |        |   |       |
|     |      |             |         |           |       |   |        |   |       |
|     |      |             |         |           |       |   |        |   |       |
|     |      |             |         |           |       |   |        |   |       |
|     |      |             |         |           |       |   |        |   |       |
|     |      |             |         |           |       |   |        |   |       |
|     |      |             |         |           |       |   |        |   |       |
|     |      |             |         |           |       |   |        |   |       |
|     |      |             |         |           |       |   |        |   |       |
|     |      |             |         |           |       |   |        |   |       |
|     |      |             |         |           |       |   |        |   |       |
|     |      |             |         |           |       |   |        |   |       |
|     |      |             |         |           |       |   |        |   |       |
|     |      |             |         |           |       |   |        |   |       |
|     |      |             |         |           |       |   |        |   |       |

# ACCOUNTING LEDGER

**PAGE.No.**

**Account Name And Number :**

**Year : _____**                                                **Month : _____**

| No. | Date | Description | Account | Reference | Debit | − | Credit | + | Total |
|-----|------|-------------|---------|-----------|-------|---|--------|---|-------|
|     |      |             |         |           |       |   |        |   |       |
|     |      |             |         |           |       |   |        |   |       |
|     |      |             |         |           |       |   |        |   |       |
|     |      |             |         |           |       |   |        |   |       |
|     |      |             |         |           |       |   |        |   |       |
|     |      |             |         |           |       |   |        |   |       |
|     |      |             |         |           |       |   |        |   |       |
|     |      |             |         |           |       |   |        |   |       |
|     |      |             |         |           |       |   |        |   |       |
|     |      |             |         |           |       |   |        |   |       |
|     |      |             |         |           |       |   |        |   |       |
|     |      |             |         |           |       |   |        |   |       |
|     |      |             |         |           |       |   |        |   |       |
|     |      |             |         |           |       |   |        |   |       |
|     |      |             |         |           |       |   |        |   |       |
|     |      |             |         |           |       |   |        |   |       |
|     |      |             |         |           |       |   |        |   |       |
|     |      |             |         |           |       |   |        |   |       |
|     |      |             |         |           |       |   |        |   |       |
|     |      |             |         |           |       |   |        |   |       |
|     |      |             |         |           |       |   |        |   |       |
|     |      |             |         |           |       |   |        |   |       |
|     |      |             |         |           |       |   |        |   |       |
|     |      |             |         |           |       |   |        |   |       |
|     |      |             |         |           |       |   |        |   |       |
|     |      |             |         |           |       |   |        |   |       |
|     |      |             |         |           |       |   |        |   |       |
|     |      |             |         |           |       |   |        |   |       |
|     |      |             |         |           |       |   |        |   |       |

# ACCOUNTING LEDGER

**PAGE.No.**

**Account Name And Number :**

**Year : _____**                                            **Month : _____**

| No. | Date | Description | Account | Reference | Debit | − | Credit | + | Total |
|-----|------|-------------|---------|-----------|-------|---|--------|---|-------|
|     |      |             |         |           |       |   |        |   |       |
|     |      |             |         |           |       |   |        |   |       |
|     |      |             |         |           |       |   |        |   |       |
|     |      |             |         |           |       |   |        |   |       |
|     |      |             |         |           |       |   |        |   |       |
|     |      |             |         |           |       |   |        |   |       |
|     |      |             |         |           |       |   |        |   |       |
|     |      |             |         |           |       |   |        |   |       |
|     |      |             |         |           |       |   |        |   |       |
|     |      |             |         |           |       |   |        |   |       |
|     |      |             |         |           |       |   |        |   |       |
|     |      |             |         |           |       |   |        |   |       |
|     |      |             |         |           |       |   |        |   |       |
|     |      |             |         |           |       |   |        |   |       |
|     |      |             |         |           |       |   |        |   |       |
|     |      |             |         |           |       |   |        |   |       |
|     |      |             |         |           |       |   |        |   |       |
|     |      |             |         |           |       |   |        |   |       |
|     |      |             |         |           |       |   |        |   |       |
|     |      |             |         |           |       |   |        |   |       |
|     |      |             |         |           |       |   |        |   |       |
|     |      |             |         |           |       |   |        |   |       |
|     |      |             |         |           |       |   |        |   |       |
|     |      |             |         |           |       |   |        |   |       |
|     |      |             |         |           |       |   |        |   |       |
|     |      |             |         |           |       |   |        |   |       |
|     |      |             |         |           |       |   |        |   |       |
|     |      |             |         |           |       |   |        |   |       |

# ACCOUNTING LEDGER

| PAGE.No. |
| --- |

**Account Name And Number :**

**Year :** _____        **Month :** _____

| No. | Date | Description | Account | Reference | Debit | − | Credit | + | Total |
| --- | --- | --- | --- | --- | --- | --- | --- | --- | --- |
| | | | | | | | | | |
| | | | | | | | | | |
| | | | | | | | | | |
| | | | | | | | | | |
| | | | | | | | | | |
| | | | | | | | | | |
| | | | | | | | | | |
| | | | | | | | | | |
| | | | | | | | | | |
| | | | | | | | | | |
| | | | | | | | | | |
| | | | | | | | | | |
| | | | | | | | | | |
| | | | | | | | | | |
| | | | | | | | | | |
| | | | | | | | | | |
| | | | | | | | | | |
| | | | | | | | | | |
| | | | | | | | | | |
| | | | | | | | | | |
| | | | | | | | | | |
| | | | | | | | | | |
| | | | | | | | | | |
| | | | | | | | | | |
| | | | | | | | | | |
| | | | | | | | | | |
| | | | | | | | | | |
| | | | | | | | | | |

# ACCOUNTING LEDGER

PAGE.No.

**Account Name And Number :**

**Year :** _____    **Month :** _____

| No. | Date | Description | Account | Reference | Debit | − | Credit | + | Total |
|-----|------|-------------|---------|-----------|-------|---|--------|---|-------|
| | | | | | | | | | |
| | | | | | | | | | |
| | | | | | | | | | |
| | | | | | | | | | |
| | | | | | | | | | |
| | | | | | | | | | |
| | | | | | | | | | |
| | | | | | | | | | |
| | | | | | | | | | |
| | | | | | | | | | |
| | | | | | | | | | |
| | | | | | | | | | |
| | | | | | | | | | |
| | | | | | | | | | |
| | | | | | | | | | |
| | | | | | | | | | |
| | | | | | | | | | |
| | | | | | | | | | |
| | | | | | | | | | |
| | | | | | | | | | |
| | | | | | | | | | |
| | | | | | | | | | |
| | | | | | | | | | |
| | | | | | | | | | |
| | | | | | | | | | |
| | | | | | | | | | |
| | | | | | | | | | |
| | | | | | | | | | |

# ACCOUNTING LEDGER

PAGE.No.

**Account Name And Number :**

**Year : _____**                                    **Month : _____**

| No. | Date | Description | Account | Reference | Debit | — | Credit | + | Total |
|-----|------|-------------|---------|-----------|-------|---|--------|---|-------|
|     |      |             |         |           |       |   |        |   |       |
|     |      |             |         |           |       |   |        |   |       |
|     |      |             |         |           |       |   |        |   |       |
|     |      |             |         |           |       |   |        |   |       |
|     |      |             |         |           |       |   |        |   |       |
|     |      |             |         |           |       |   |        |   |       |
|     |      |             |         |           |       |   |        |   |       |
|     |      |             |         |           |       |   |        |   |       |
|     |      |             |         |           |       |   |        |   |       |
|     |      |             |         |           |       |   |        |   |       |
|     |      |             |         |           |       |   |        |   |       |
|     |      |             |         |           |       |   |        |   |       |
|     |      |             |         |           |       |   |        |   |       |
|     |      |             |         |           |       |   |        |   |       |
|     |      |             |         |           |       |   |        |   |       |
|     |      |             |         |           |       |   |        |   |       |
|     |      |             |         |           |       |   |        |   |       |
|     |      |             |         |           |       |   |        |   |       |
|     |      |             |         |           |       |   |        |   |       |
|     |      |             |         |           |       |   |        |   |       |
|     |      |             |         |           |       |   |        |   |       |
|     |      |             |         |           |       |   |        |   |       |
|     |      |             |         |           |       |   |        |   |       |
|     |      |             |         |           |       |   |        |   |       |
|     |      |             |         |           |       |   |        |   |       |
|     |      |             |         |           |       |   |        |   |       |
|     |      |             |         |           |       |   |        |   |       |
|     |      |             |         |           |       |   |        |   |       |
|     |      |             |         |           |       |   |        |   |       |
|     |      |             |         |           |       |   |        |   |       |

# ACCOUNTING LEDGER

**PAGE.No.**

**Account Name And Number :**

**Year : _____**

**Month : _____**

| No. | Date | Description | Account | Reference | Debit | − | Credit | + | Total |
|-----|------|-------------|---------|-----------|-------|---|--------|---|-------|
| | | | | | | | | | |
| | | | | | | | | | |
| | | | | | | | | | |
| | | | | | | | | | |
| | | | | | | | | | |
| | | | | | | | | | |
| | | | | | | | | | |
| | | | | | | | | | |
| | | | | | | | | | |
| | | | | | | | | | |
| | | | | | | | | | |
| | | | | | | | | | |
| | | | | | | | | | |
| | | | | | | | | | |
| | | | | | | | | | |
| | | | | | | | | | |
| | | | | | | | | | |
| | | | | | | | | | |
| | | | | | | | | | |
| | | | | | | | | | |
| | | | | | | | | | |
| | | | | | | | | | |
| | | | | | | | | | |
| | | | | | | | | | |
| | | | | | | | | | |
| | | | | | | | | | |
| | | | | | | | | | |
| | | | | | | | | | |
| | | | | | | | | | |

# ACCOUNTING LEDGER

PAGE.No.

Account Name And Number :

Year : _____                                    Month : _____

| No. | Date | Description | Account | Reference | Debit | − | Credit | + | Total |
|-----|------|-------------|---------|-----------|-------|---|--------|---|-------|
|     |      |             |         |           |       |   |        |   |       |
|     |      |             |         |           |       |   |        |   |       |
|     |      |             |         |           |       |   |        |   |       |
|     |      |             |         |           |       |   |        |   |       |
|     |      |             |         |           |       |   |        |   |       |
|     |      |             |         |           |       |   |        |   |       |
|     |      |             |         |           |       |   |        |   |       |
|     |      |             |         |           |       |   |        |   |       |
|     |      |             |         |           |       |   |        |   |       |
|     |      |             |         |           |       |   |        |   |       |
|     |      |             |         |           |       |   |        |   |       |
|     |      |             |         |           |       |   |        |   |       |
|     |      |             |         |           |       |   |        |   |       |
|     |      |             |         |           |       |   |        |   |       |
|     |      |             |         |           |       |   |        |   |       |
|     |      |             |         |           |       |   |        |   |       |
|     |      |             |         |           |       |   |        |   |       |
|     |      |             |         |           |       |   |        |   |       |
|     |      |             |         |           |       |   |        |   |       |
|     |      |             |         |           |       |   |        |   |       |
|     |      |             |         |           |       |   |        |   |       |
|     |      |             |         |           |       |   |        |   |       |
|     |      |             |         |           |       |   |        |   |       |
|     |      |             |         |           |       |   |        |   |       |
|     |      |             |         |           |       |   |        |   |       |
|     |      |             |         |           |       |   |        |   |       |
|     |      |             |         |           |       |   |        |   |       |
|     |      |             |         |           |       |   |        |   |       |
|     |      |             |         |           |       |   |        |   |       |

# ACCOUNTING LEDGER

PAGE.No.

**Account Name And Number :**

**Year :** _____                              **Month :** _____

| No. | Date | Description | Account | Reference | Debit | − | Credit | + | Total |
|-----|------|-------------|---------|-----------|-------|---|--------|---|-------|
|     |      |             |         |           |       |   |        |   |       |
|     |      |             |         |           |       |   |        |   |       |
|     |      |             |         |           |       |   |        |   |       |
|     |      |             |         |           |       |   |        |   |       |
|     |      |             |         |           |       |   |        |   |       |
|     |      |             |         |           |       |   |        |   |       |
|     |      |             |         |           |       |   |        |   |       |
|     |      |             |         |           |       |   |        |   |       |
|     |      |             |         |           |       |   |        |   |       |
|     |      |             |         |           |       |   |        |   |       |
|     |      |             |         |           |       |   |        |   |       |
|     |      |             |         |           |       |   |        |   |       |
|     |      |             |         |           |       |   |        |   |       |
|     |      |             |         |           |       |   |        |   |       |
|     |      |             |         |           |       |   |        |   |       |
|     |      |             |         |           |       |   |        |   |       |
|     |      |             |         |           |       |   |        |   |       |
|     |      |             |         |           |       |   |        |   |       |
|     |      |             |         |           |       |   |        |   |       |
|     |      |             |         |           |       |   |        |   |       |
|     |      |             |         |           |       |   |        |   |       |
|     |      |             |         |           |       |   |        |   |       |
|     |      |             |         |           |       |   |        |   |       |
|     |      |             |         |           |       |   |        |   |       |
|     |      |             |         |           |       |   |        |   |       |
|     |      |             |         |           |       |   |        |   |       |
|     |      |             |         |           |       |   |        |   |       |

# ACCOUNTING LEDGER

## PAGE.No.

**Account Name And Number :**

**Year : _____**                    **Month : _____**

| No. | Date | Description | Account | Reference | Debit | − | Credit | + | Total |
|-----|------|-------------|---------|-----------|-------|---|--------|---|-------|
|     |      |             |         |           |       |   |        |   |       |
|     |      |             |         |           |       |   |        |   |       |
|     |      |             |         |           |       |   |        |   |       |
|     |      |             |         |           |       |   |        |   |       |
|     |      |             |         |           |       |   |        |   |       |
|     |      |             |         |           |       |   |        |   |       |
|     |      |             |         |           |       |   |        |   |       |
|     |      |             |         |           |       |   |        |   |       |
|     |      |             |         |           |       |   |        |   |       |
|     |      |             |         |           |       |   |        |   |       |
|     |      |             |         |           |       |   |        |   |       |
|     |      |             |         |           |       |   |        |   |       |
|     |      |             |         |           |       |   |        |   |       |
|     |      |             |         |           |       |   |        |   |       |
|     |      |             |         |           |       |   |        |   |       |
|     |      |             |         |           |       |   |        |   |       |
|     |      |             |         |           |       |   |        |   |       |
|     |      |             |         |           |       |   |        |   |       |
|     |      |             |         |           |       |   |        |   |       |
|     |      |             |         |           |       |   |        |   |       |
|     |      |             |         |           |       |   |        |   |       |
|     |      |             |         |           |       |   |        |   |       |
|     |      |             |         |           |       |   |        |   |       |
|     |      |             |         |           |       |   |        |   |       |
|     |      |             |         |           |       |   |        |   |       |
|     |      |             |         |           |       |   |        |   |       |
|     |      |             |         |           |       |   |        |   |       |
|     |      |             |         |           |       |   |        |   |       |
|     |      |             |         |           |       |   |        |   |       |
|     |      |             |         |           |       |   |        |   |       |

# ACCOUNTING LEDGER

**PAGE.No.**

Account Name And Number :

Year : _____

Month : _____

| No. | Date | Description | Account | Reference | Debit | − | Credit | + | Total |
|-----|------|-------------|---------|-----------|-------|---|--------|---|-------|
|     |      |             |         |           |       |   |        |   |       |
|     |      |             |         |           |       |   |        |   |       |
|     |      |             |         |           |       |   |        |   |       |
|     |      |             |         |           |       |   |        |   |       |
|     |      |             |         |           |       |   |        |   |       |
|     |      |             |         |           |       |   |        |   |       |
|     |      |             |         |           |       |   |        |   |       |
|     |      |             |         |           |       |   |        |   |       |
|     |      |             |         |           |       |   |        |   |       |
|     |      |             |         |           |       |   |        |   |       |
|     |      |             |         |           |       |   |        |   |       |
|     |      |             |         |           |       |   |        |   |       |
|     |      |             |         |           |       |   |        |   |       |
|     |      |             |         |           |       |   |        |   |       |
|     |      |             |         |           |       |   |        |   |       |
|     |      |             |         |           |       |   |        |   |       |
|     |      |             |         |           |       |   |        |   |       |
|     |      |             |         |           |       |   |        |   |       |
|     |      |             |         |           |       |   |        |   |       |
|     |      |             |         |           |       |   |        |   |       |
|     |      |             |         |           |       |   |        |   |       |
|     |      |             |         |           |       |   |        |   |       |
|     |      |             |         |           |       |   |        |   |       |
|     |      |             |         |           |       |   |        |   |       |
|     |      |             |         |           |       |   |        |   |       |
|     |      |             |         |           |       |   |        |   |       |
|     |      |             |         |           |       |   |        |   |       |

# ACCOUNTING LEDGER

**PAGE.No.**

**Account Name And Number :**

**Year : _____**                                    **Month : _____**

| No. | Date | Description | Account | Reference | Debit | − | Credit | + | Total |
|-----|------|-------------|---------|-----------|-------|---|--------|---|-------|
|     |      |             |         |           |       |   |        |   |       |
|     |      |             |         |           |       |   |        |   |       |
|     |      |             |         |           |       |   |        |   |       |
|     |      |             |         |           |       |   |        |   |       |
|     |      |             |         |           |       |   |        |   |       |
|     |      |             |         |           |       |   |        |   |       |
|     |      |             |         |           |       |   |        |   |       |
|     |      |             |         |           |       |   |        |   |       |
|     |      |             |         |           |       |   |        |   |       |
|     |      |             |         |           |       |   |        |   |       |
|     |      |             |         |           |       |   |        |   |       |
|     |      |             |         |           |       |   |        |   |       |
|     |      |             |         |           |       |   |        |   |       |
|     |      |             |         |           |       |   |        |   |       |
|     |      |             |         |           |       |   |        |   |       |
|     |      |             |         |           |       |   |        |   |       |
|     |      |             |         |           |       |   |        |   |       |
|     |      |             |         |           |       |   |        |   |       |
|     |      |             |         |           |       |   |        |   |       |
|     |      |             |         |           |       |   |        |   |       |
|     |      |             |         |           |       |   |        |   |       |
|     |      |             |         |           |       |   |        |   |       |
|     |      |             |         |           |       |   |        |   |       |
|     |      |             |         |           |       |   |        |   |       |
|     |      |             |         |           |       |   |        |   |       |
|     |      |             |         |           |       |   |        |   |       |
|     |      |             |         |           |       |   |        |   |       |
|     |      |             |         |           |       |   |        |   |       |

# ACCOUNTING LEDGER

PAGE.No.

**Account Name And Number :**

**Year : _____**                                          **Month : _____**

| No. | Date | Description | Account | Reference | Debit | − | Credit | + | Total |
|-----|------|-------------|---------|-----------|-------|---|--------|---|-------|
| | | | | | | | | | |
| | | | | | | | | | |
| | | | | | | | | | |
| | | | | | | | | | |
| | | | | | | | | | |
| | | | | | | | | | |
| | | | | | | | | | |
| | | | | | | | | | |
| | | | | | | | | | |
| | | | | | | | | | |
| | | | | | | | | | |
| | | | | | | | | | |
| | | | | | | | | | |
| | | | | | | | | | |
| | | | | | | | | | |
| | | | | | | | | | |
| | | | | | | | | | |
| | | | | | | | | | |
| | | | | | | | | | |
| | | | | | | | | | |
| | | | | | | | | | |
| | | | | | | | | | |
| | | | | | | | | | |
| | | | | | | | | | |
| | | | | | | | | | |
| | | | | | | | | | |
| | | | | | | | | | |
| | | | | | | | | | |
| | | | | | | | | | |

# ACCOUNTING LEDGER

**PAGE.No.**

**Account Name And Number :**

**Year : _____**                               **Month : _____**

| No. | Date | Description | Account | Reference | Debit | − | Credit | + | Total |
|-----|------|-------------|---------|-----------|-------|---|--------|---|-------|
|     |      |             |         |           |       |   |        |   |       |
|     |      |             |         |           |       |   |        |   |       |
|     |      |             |         |           |       |   |        |   |       |
|     |      |             |         |           |       |   |        |   |       |
|     |      |             |         |           |       |   |        |   |       |
|     |      |             |         |           |       |   |        |   |       |
|     |      |             |         |           |       |   |        |   |       |
|     |      |             |         |           |       |   |        |   |       |
|     |      |             |         |           |       |   |        |   |       |
|     |      |             |         |           |       |   |        |   |       |
|     |      |             |         |           |       |   |        |   |       |
|     |      |             |         |           |       |   |        |   |       |
|     |      |             |         |           |       |   |        |   |       |
|     |      |             |         |           |       |   |        |   |       |
|     |      |             |         |           |       |   |        |   |       |
|     |      |             |         |           |       |   |        |   |       |
|     |      |             |         |           |       |   |        |   |       |
|     |      |             |         |           |       |   |        |   |       |
|     |      |             |         |           |       |   |        |   |       |
|     |      |             |         |           |       |   |        |   |       |
|     |      |             |         |           |       |   |        |   |       |
|     |      |             |         |           |       |   |        |   |       |
|     |      |             |         |           |       |   |        |   |       |
|     |      |             |         |           |       |   |        |   |       |
|     |      |             |         |           |       |   |        |   |       |
|     |      |             |         |           |       |   |        |   |       |
|     |      |             |         |           |       |   |        |   |       |
|     |      |             |         |           |       |   |        |   |       |
|     |      |             |         |           |       |   |        |   |       |
|     |      |             |         |           |       |   |        |   |       |
|     |      |             |         |           |       |   |        |   |       |

# ACCOUNTING LEDGER

PAGE.No.

**Account Name And Number :**

**Year : _____**                                          **Month : _____**

| No. | Date | Description | Account | Reference | Debit | − | Credit | + | Total |
|-----|------|-------------|---------|-----------|-------|---|--------|---|-------|
|     |      |             |         |           |       |   |        |   |       |
|     |      |             |         |           |       |   |        |   |       |
|     |      |             |         |           |       |   |        |   |       |
|     |      |             |         |           |       |   |        |   |       |
|     |      |             |         |           |       |   |        |   |       |
|     |      |             |         |           |       |   |        |   |       |
|     |      |             |         |           |       |   |        |   |       |
|     |      |             |         |           |       |   |        |   |       |
|     |      |             |         |           |       |   |        |   |       |
|     |      |             |         |           |       |   |        |   |       |
|     |      |             |         |           |       |   |        |   |       |
|     |      |             |         |           |       |   |        |   |       |
|     |      |             |         |           |       |   |        |   |       |
|     |      |             |         |           |       |   |        |   |       |
|     |      |             |         |           |       |   |        |   |       |
|     |      |             |         |           |       |   |        |   |       |
|     |      |             |         |           |       |   |        |   |       |
|     |      |             |         |           |       |   |        |   |       |
|     |      |             |         |           |       |   |        |   |       |
|     |      |             |         |           |       |   |        |   |       |
|     |      |             |         |           |       |   |        |   |       |
|     |      |             |         |           |       |   |        |   |       |
|     |      |             |         |           |       |   |        |   |       |
|     |      |             |         |           |       |   |        |   |       |
|     |      |             |         |           |       |   |        |   |       |
|     |      |             |         |           |       |   |        |   |       |

# ACCOUNTING LEDGER

**PAGE.No.**

Account Name And Number :

Year : _____                                    Month : _____

| No. | Date | Description | Account | Reference | Debit | − | Credit | + | Total |
|-----|------|-------------|---------|-----------|-------|---|--------|---|-------|
|     |      |             |         |           |       |   |        |   |       |
|     |      |             |         |           |       |   |        |   |       |
|     |      |             |         |           |       |   |        |   |       |
|     |      |             |         |           |       |   |        |   |       |
|     |      |             |         |           |       |   |        |   |       |
|     |      |             |         |           |       |   |        |   |       |
|     |      |             |         |           |       |   |        |   |       |
|     |      |             |         |           |       |   |        |   |       |
|     |      |             |         |           |       |   |        |   |       |
|     |      |             |         |           |       |   |        |   |       |
|     |      |             |         |           |       |   |        |   |       |
|     |      |             |         |           |       |   |        |   |       |
|     |      |             |         |           |       |   |        |   |       |
|     |      |             |         |           |       |   |        |   |       |
|     |      |             |         |           |       |   |        |   |       |
|     |      |             |         |           |       |   |        |   |       |
|     |      |             |         |           |       |   |        |   |       |
|     |      |             |         |           |       |   |        |   |       |
|     |      |             |         |           |       |   |        |   |       |
|     |      |             |         |           |       |   |        |   |       |
|     |      |             |         |           |       |   |        |   |       |
|     |      |             |         |           |       |   |        |   |       |
|     |      |             |         |           |       |   |        |   |       |
|     |      |             |         |           |       |   |        |   |       |
|     |      |             |         |           |       |   |        |   |       |
|     |      |             |         |           |       |   |        |   |       |
|     |      |             |         |           |       |   |        |   |       |
|     |      |             |         |           |       |   |        |   |       |

# ACCOUNTING LEDGER

**PAGE.No.**

**Account Name And Number :**

**Year : _____**                                    **Month : _____**

| No. | Date | Description | Account | Reference | Debit | − | Credit | + | Total |
|-----|------|-------------|---------|-----------|-------|---|--------|---|-------|
|     |      |             |         |           |       |   |        |   |       |
|     |      |             |         |           |       |   |        |   |       |
|     |      |             |         |           |       |   |        |   |       |
|     |      |             |         |           |       |   |        |   |       |
|     |      |             |         |           |       |   |        |   |       |
|     |      |             |         |           |       |   |        |   |       |
|     |      |             |         |           |       |   |        |   |       |
|     |      |             |         |           |       |   |        |   |       |
|     |      |             |         |           |       |   |        |   |       |
|     |      |             |         |           |       |   |        |   |       |
|     |      |             |         |           |       |   |        |   |       |
|     |      |             |         |           |       |   |        |   |       |
|     |      |             |         |           |       |   |        |   |       |
|     |      |             |         |           |       |   |        |   |       |
|     |      |             |         |           |       |   |        |   |       |
|     |      |             |         |           |       |   |        |   |       |
|     |      |             |         |           |       |   |        |   |       |
|     |      |             |         |           |       |   |        |   |       |
|     |      |             |         |           |       |   |        |   |       |
|     |      |             |         |           |       |   |        |   |       |
|     |      |             |         |           |       |   |        |   |       |
|     |      |             |         |           |       |   |        |   |       |
|     |      |             |         |           |       |   |        |   |       |
|     |      |             |         |           |       |   |        |   |       |
|     |      |             |         |           |       |   |        |   |       |
|     |      |             |         |           |       |   |        |   |       |
|     |      |             |         |           |       |   |        |   |       |

# ACCOUNTING LEDGER

**PAGE.No.**

**Account Name And Number :**

**Year :** ____    **Month :** ____

| No. | Date | Description | Account | Reference | Debit | − | Credit | + | Total |
|-----|------|-------------|---------|-----------|-------|---|--------|---|-------|
|     |      |             |         |           |       |   |        |   |       |
|     |      |             |         |           |       |   |        |   |       |
|     |      |             |         |           |       |   |        |   |       |
|     |      |             |         |           |       |   |        |   |       |
|     |      |             |         |           |       |   |        |   |       |
|     |      |             |         |           |       |   |        |   |       |
|     |      |             |         |           |       |   |        |   |       |
|     |      |             |         |           |       |   |        |   |       |
|     |      |             |         |           |       |   |        |   |       |
|     |      |             |         |           |       |   |        |   |       |
|     |      |             |         |           |       |   |        |   |       |
|     |      |             |         |           |       |   |        |   |       |
|     |      |             |         |           |       |   |        |   |       |
|     |      |             |         |           |       |   |        |   |       |
|     |      |             |         |           |       |   |        |   |       |
|     |      |             |         |           |       |   |        |   |       |
|     |      |             |         |           |       |   |        |   |       |
|     |      |             |         |           |       |   |        |   |       |
|     |      |             |         |           |       |   |        |   |       |
|     |      |             |         |           |       |   |        |   |       |
|     |      |             |         |           |       |   |        |   |       |
|     |      |             |         |           |       |   |        |   |       |
|     |      |             |         |           |       |   |        |   |       |
|     |      |             |         |           |       |   |        |   |       |
|     |      |             |         |           |       |   |        |   |       |
|     |      |             |         |           |       |   |        |   |       |
|     |      |             |         |           |       |   |        |   |       |
|     |      |             |         |           |       |   |        |   |       |
|     |      |             |         |           |       |   |        |   |       |

# ACCOUNTING LEDGER

PAGE.No.

**Account Name And Number :**

**Year :** _____      **Month :** _____

| No. | Date | Description | Account | Reference | Debit | − | Credit | + | Total |
|-----|------|-------------|---------|-----------|-------|---|--------|---|-------|
| | | | | | | | | | |
| | | | | | | | | | |
| | | | | | | | | | |
| | | | | | | | | | |
| | | | | | | | | | |
| | | | | | | | | | |
| | | | | | | | | | |
| | | | | | | | | | |
| | | | | | | | | | |
| | | | | | | | | | |
| | | | | | | | | | |
| | | | | | | | | | |
| | | | | | | | | | |
| | | | | | | | | | |
| | | | | | | | | | |
| | | | | | | | | | |
| | | | | | | | | | |
| | | | | | | | | | |
| | | | | | | | | | |
| | | | | | | | | | |
| | | | | | | | | | |
| | | | | | | | | | |
| | | | | | | | | | |
| | | | | | | | | | |
| | | | | | | | | | |
| | | | | | | | | | |
| | | | | | | | | | |
| | | | | | | | | | |

# ACCOUNTING LEDGER

**PAGE.No.**

**Account Name And Number :**

**Year :** ____    **Month :** ____

| No. | Date | Description | Account | Reference | Debit | − | Credit | + | Total |
|-----|------|-------------|---------|-----------|-------|---|--------|---|-------|
| | | | | | | | | | |
| | | | | | | | | | |
| | | | | | | | | | |
| | | | | | | | | | |
| | | | | | | | | | |
| | | | | | | | | | |
| | | | | | | | | | |
| | | | | | | | | | |
| | | | | | | | | | |
| | | | | | | | | | |
| | | | | | | | | | |
| | | | | | | | | | |
| | | | | | | | | | |
| | | | | | | | | | |
| | | | | | | | | | |
| | | | | | | | | | |
| | | | | | | | | | |
| | | | | | | | | | |
| | | | | | | | | | |
| | | | | | | | | | |
| | | | | | | | | | |
| | | | | | | | | | |
| | | | | | | | | | |
| | | | | | | | | | |
| | | | | | | | | | |
| | | | | | | | | | |
| | | | | | | | | | |
| | | | | | | | | | |

# ACCOUNTING LEDGER

PAGE.No.

Account Name And Number :

Year : _____                                         Month : _____

| No. | Date | Description | Account | Reference | Debit | − | Credit | + | Total |
|-----|------|-------------|---------|-----------|-------|---|--------|---|-------|
|     |      |             |         |           |       |   |        |   |       |
|     |      |             |         |           |       |   |        |   |       |
|     |      |             |         |           |       |   |        |   |       |
|     |      |             |         |           |       |   |        |   |       |
|     |      |             |         |           |       |   |        |   |       |
|     |      |             |         |           |       |   |        |   |       |
|     |      |             |         |           |       |   |        |   |       |
|     |      |             |         |           |       |   |        |   |       |
|     |      |             |         |           |       |   |        |   |       |
|     |      |             |         |           |       |   |        |   |       |
|     |      |             |         |           |       |   |        |   |       |
|     |      |             |         |           |       |   |        |   |       |
|     |      |             |         |           |       |   |        |   |       |
|     |      |             |         |           |       |   |        |   |       |
|     |      |             |         |           |       |   |        |   |       |
|     |      |             |         |           |       |   |        |   |       |
|     |      |             |         |           |       |   |        |   |       |
|     |      |             |         |           |       |   |        |   |       |
|     |      |             |         |           |       |   |        |   |       |
|     |      |             |         |           |       |   |        |   |       |
|     |      |             |         |           |       |   |        |   |       |
|     |      |             |         |           |       |   |        |   |       |
|     |      |             |         |           |       |   |        |   |       |
|     |      |             |         |           |       |   |        |   |       |
|     |      |             |         |           |       |   |        |   |       |

# ACCOUNTING LEDGER

PAGE.No.

Account Name And Number :

Year : _____          Month : _____

| No. | Date | Description | Account | Reference | Debit | − | Credit | + | Total |
|-----|------|-------------|---------|-----------|-------|---|--------|---|-------|
|     |      |             |         |           |       |   |        |   |       |
|     |      |             |         |           |       |   |        |   |       |
|     |      |             |         |           |       |   |        |   |       |
|     |      |             |         |           |       |   |        |   |       |
|     |      |             |         |           |       |   |        |   |       |
|     |      |             |         |           |       |   |        |   |       |
|     |      |             |         |           |       |   |        |   |       |
|     |      |             |         |           |       |   |        |   |       |
|     |      |             |         |           |       |   |        |   |       |
|     |      |             |         |           |       |   |        |   |       |
|     |      |             |         |           |       |   |        |   |       |
|     |      |             |         |           |       |   |        |   |       |
|     |      |             |         |           |       |   |        |   |       |
|     |      |             |         |           |       |   |        |   |       |
|     |      |             |         |           |       |   |        |   |       |
|     |      |             |         |           |       |   |        |   |       |
|     |      |             |         |           |       |   |        |   |       |
|     |      |             |         |           |       |   |        |   |       |
|     |      |             |         |           |       |   |        |   |       |
|     |      |             |         |           |       |   |        |   |       |
|     |      |             |         |           |       |   |        |   |       |
|     |      |             |         |           |       |   |        |   |       |
|     |      |             |         |           |       |   |        |   |       |
|     |      |             |         |           |       |   |        |   |       |
|     |      |             |         |           |       |   |        |   |       |
|     |      |             |         |           |       |   |        |   |       |
|     |      |             |         |           |       |   |        |   |       |
|     |      |             |         |           |       |   |        |   |       |

# ACCOUNTING LEDGER

**PAGE.No.**

**Account Name And Number :**

**Year :** _____       **Month :** _____

| No. | Date | Description | Account | Reference | Debit | − | Credit | + | Total |
|-----|------|-------------|---------|-----------|-------|---|--------|---|-------|
|     |      |             |         |           |       |   |        |   |       |
|     |      |             |         |           |       |   |        |   |       |
|     |      |             |         |           |       |   |        |   |       |
|     |      |             |         |           |       |   |        |   |       |
|     |      |             |         |           |       |   |        |   |       |
|     |      |             |         |           |       |   |        |   |       |
|     |      |             |         |           |       |   |        |   |       |
|     |      |             |         |           |       |   |        |   |       |
|     |      |             |         |           |       |   |        |   |       |
|     |      |             |         |           |       |   |        |   |       |
|     |      |             |         |           |       |   |        |   |       |
|     |      |             |         |           |       |   |        |   |       |
|     |      |             |         |           |       |   |        |   |       |
|     |      |             |         |           |       |   |        |   |       |
|     |      |             |         |           |       |   |        |   |       |
|     |      |             |         |           |       |   |        |   |       |
|     |      |             |         |           |       |   |        |   |       |
|     |      |             |         |           |       |   |        |   |       |
|     |      |             |         |           |       |   |        |   |       |
|     |      |             |         |           |       |   |        |   |       |
|     |      |             |         |           |       |   |        |   |       |
|     |      |             |         |           |       |   |        |   |       |
|     |      |             |         |           |       |   |        |   |       |
|     |      |             |         |           |       |   |        |   |       |
|     |      |             |         |           |       |   |        |   |       |
|     |      |             |         |           |       |   |        |   |       |
|     |      |             |         |           |       |   |        |   |       |
|     |      |             |         |           |       |   |        |   |       |

# ACCOUNTING LEDGER

**PAGE.No.**

**Account Name And Number :**

**Year : _____**          **Month : _____**

| No. | Date | Description | Account | Reference | Debit | − | Credit | + | Total |
|-----|------|-------------|---------|-----------|-------|---|--------|---|-------|
|     |      |             |         |           |       |   |        |   |       |
|     |      |             |         |           |       |   |        |   |       |
|     |      |             |         |           |       |   |        |   |       |
|     |      |             |         |           |       |   |        |   |       |
|     |      |             |         |           |       |   |        |   |       |
|     |      |             |         |           |       |   |        |   |       |
|     |      |             |         |           |       |   |        |   |       |
|     |      |             |         |           |       |   |        |   |       |
|     |      |             |         |           |       |   |        |   |       |
|     |      |             |         |           |       |   |        |   |       |
|     |      |             |         |           |       |   |        |   |       |
|     |      |             |         |           |       |   |        |   |       |
|     |      |             |         |           |       |   |        |   |       |
|     |      |             |         |           |       |   |        |   |       |
|     |      |             |         |           |       |   |        |   |       |
|     |      |             |         |           |       |   |        |   |       |
|     |      |             |         |           |       |   |        |   |       |
|     |      |             |         |           |       |   |        |   |       |
|     |      |             |         |           |       |   |        |   |       |
|     |      |             |         |           |       |   |        |   |       |
|     |      |             |         |           |       |   |        |   |       |
|     |      |             |         |           |       |   |        |   |       |
|     |      |             |         |           |       |   |        |   |       |
|     |      |             |         |           |       |   |        |   |       |
|     |      |             |         |           |       |   |        |   |       |

# ACCOUNTING LEDGER

PAGE.No.

**Account Name And Number :**

**Year :** ____                                      **Month :** ____

| No. | Date | Description | Account | Reference | Debit | − | Credit | + | Total |
|-----|------|-------------|---------|-----------|-------|---|--------|---|-------|
| | | | | | | | | | |
| | | | | | | | | | |
| | | | | | | | | | |
| | | | | | | | | | |
| | | | | | | | | | |
| | | | | | | | | | |
| | | | | | | | | | |
| | | | | | | | | | |
| | | | | | | | | | |
| | | | | | | | | | |
| | | | | | | | | | |
| | | | | | | | | | |
| | | | | | | | | | |
| | | | | | | | | | |
| | | | | | | | | | |
| | | | | | | | | | |
| | | | | | | | | | |
| | | | | | | | | | |
| | | | | | | | | | |
| | | | | | | | | | |
| | | | | | | | | | |
| | | | | | | | | | |
| | | | | | | | | | |
| | | | | | | | | | |
| | | | | | | | | | |
| | | | | | | | | | |

# ACCOUNTING LEDGER

**PAGE.No.**

**Account Name And Number :**

**Year :** _____                                          **Month :** _____

| No. | Date | Description | Account | Reference | Debit | − | Credit | + | Total |
|-----|------|-------------|---------|-----------|-------|---|--------|---|-------|
|     |      |             |         |           |       |   |        |   |       |
|     |      |             |         |           |       |   |        |   |       |
|     |      |             |         |           |       |   |        |   |       |
|     |      |             |         |           |       |   |        |   |       |
|     |      |             |         |           |       |   |        |   |       |
|     |      |             |         |           |       |   |        |   |       |
|     |      |             |         |           |       |   |        |   |       |
|     |      |             |         |           |       |   |        |   |       |
|     |      |             |         |           |       |   |        |   |       |
|     |      |             |         |           |       |   |        |   |       |
|     |      |             |         |           |       |   |        |   |       |
|     |      |             |         |           |       |   |        |   |       |
|     |      |             |         |           |       |   |        |   |       |
|     |      |             |         |           |       |   |        |   |       |
|     |      |             |         |           |       |   |        |   |       |
|     |      |             |         |           |       |   |        |   |       |
|     |      |             |         |           |       |   |        |   |       |
|     |      |             |         |           |       |   |        |   |       |
|     |      |             |         |           |       |   |        |   |       |
|     |      |             |         |           |       |   |        |   |       |
|     |      |             |         |           |       |   |        |   |       |
|     |      |             |         |           |       |   |        |   |       |
|     |      |             |         |           |       |   |        |   |       |
|     |      |             |         |           |       |   |        |   |       |
|     |      |             |         |           |       |   |        |   |       |
|     |      |             |         |           |       |   |        |   |       |
|     |      |             |         |           |       |   |        |   |       |
|     |      |             |         |           |       |   |        |   |       |
|     |      |             |         |           |       |   |        |   |       |
|     |      |             |         |           |       |   |        |   |       |

# ACCOUNTING LEDGER

**PAGE.No.**

**Account Name And Number :**

**Year :** _____          **Month :** _____

| No. | Date | Description | Account | Reference | Debit | − | Credit | + | Total |
|-----|------|-------------|---------|-----------|-------|---|--------|---|-------|
|     |      |             |         |           |       |   |        |   |       |
|     |      |             |         |           |       |   |        |   |       |
|     |      |             |         |           |       |   |        |   |       |
|     |      |             |         |           |       |   |        |   |       |
|     |      |             |         |           |       |   |        |   |       |
|     |      |             |         |           |       |   |        |   |       |
|     |      |             |         |           |       |   |        |   |       |
|     |      |             |         |           |       |   |        |   |       |
|     |      |             |         |           |       |   |        |   |       |
|     |      |             |         |           |       |   |        |   |       |
|     |      |             |         |           |       |   |        |   |       |
|     |      |             |         |           |       |   |        |   |       |
|     |      |             |         |           |       |   |        |   |       |
|     |      |             |         |           |       |   |        |   |       |
|     |      |             |         |           |       |   |        |   |       |
|     |      |             |         |           |       |   |        |   |       |
|     |      |             |         |           |       |   |        |   |       |
|     |      |             |         |           |       |   |        |   |       |
|     |      |             |         |           |       |   |        |   |       |
|     |      |             |         |           |       |   |        |   |       |
|     |      |             |         |           |       |   |        |   |       |
|     |      |             |         |           |       |   |        |   |       |
|     |      |             |         |           |       |   |        |   |       |
|     |      |             |         |           |       |   |        |   |       |
|     |      |             |         |           |       |   |        |   |       |
|     |      |             |         |           |       |   |        |   |       |
|     |      |             |         |           |       |   |        |   |       |
|     |      |             |         |           |       |   |        |   |       |

# ACCOUNTING LEDGER

PAGE.No.

Account Name And Number :

Year : _____                                    Month : _____

| No. | Date | Description | Account | Reference | Debit | − | Credit | + | Total |
|---|---|---|---|---|---|---|---|---|---|
| | | | | | | | | | |
| | | | | | | | | | |
| | | | | | | | | | |
| | | | | | | | | | |
| | | | | | | | | | |
| | | | | | | | | | |
| | | | | | | | | | |
| | | | | | | | | | |
| | | | | | | | | | |
| | | | | | | | | | |
| | | | | | | | | | |
| | | | | | | | | | |
| | | | | | | | | | |
| | | | | | | | | | |
| | | | | | | | | | |
| | | | | | | | | | |
| | | | | | | | | | |
| | | | | | | | | | |
| | | | | | | | | | |
| | | | | | | | | | |
| | | | | | | | | | |
| | | | | | | | | | |
| | | | | | | | | | |
| | | | | | | | | | |
| | | | | | | | | | |
| | | | | | | | | | |

# ACCOUNTING LEDGER

**PAGE.No.**

**Account Name And Number :**

**Year : _____**                                    **Month : _____**

| No. | Date | Description | Account | Reference | Debit | − | Credit | + | Total |
|-----|------|-------------|---------|-----------|-------|---|--------|---|-------|
|     |      |             |         |           |       |   |        |   |       |
|     |      |             |         |           |       |   |        |   |       |
|     |      |             |         |           |       |   |        |   |       |
|     |      |             |         |           |       |   |        |   |       |
|     |      |             |         |           |       |   |        |   |       |
|     |      |             |         |           |       |   |        |   |       |
|     |      |             |         |           |       |   |        |   |       |
|     |      |             |         |           |       |   |        |   |       |
|     |      |             |         |           |       |   |        |   |       |
|     |      |             |         |           |       |   |        |   |       |
|     |      |             |         |           |       |   |        |   |       |
|     |      |             |         |           |       |   |        |   |       |
|     |      |             |         |           |       |   |        |   |       |
|     |      |             |         |           |       |   |        |   |       |
|     |      |             |         |           |       |   |        |   |       |
|     |      |             |         |           |       |   |        |   |       |
|     |      |             |         |           |       |   |        |   |       |
|     |      |             |         |           |       |   |        |   |       |
|     |      |             |         |           |       |   |        |   |       |
|     |      |             |         |           |       |   |        |   |       |
|     |      |             |         |           |       |   |        |   |       |
|     |      |             |         |           |       |   |        |   |       |
|     |      |             |         |           |       |   |        |   |       |
|     |      |             |         |           |       |   |        |   |       |
|     |      |             |         |           |       |   |        |   |       |
|     |      |             |         |           |       |   |        |   |       |
|     |      |             |         |           |       |   |        |   |       |

# ACCOUNTING LEDGER

PAGE.No.

Account Name And Number :

Year : _____                                    Month : _____

| No. | Date | Description | Account | Reference | Debit | — | Credit | + | Total |
|-----|------|-------------|---------|-----------|-------|---|--------|---|-------|
|     |      |             |         |           |       |   |        |   |       |
|     |      |             |         |           |       |   |        |   |       |
|     |      |             |         |           |       |   |        |   |       |
|     |      |             |         |           |       |   |        |   |       |
|     |      |             |         |           |       |   |        |   |       |
|     |      |             |         |           |       |   |        |   |       |
|     |      |             |         |           |       |   |        |   |       |
|     |      |             |         |           |       |   |        |   |       |
|     |      |             |         |           |       |   |        |   |       |
|     |      |             |         |           |       |   |        |   |       |
|     |      |             |         |           |       |   |        |   |       |
|     |      |             |         |           |       |   |        |   |       |
|     |      |             |         |           |       |   |        |   |       |
|     |      |             |         |           |       |   |        |   |       |
|     |      |             |         |           |       |   |        |   |       |
|     |      |             |         |           |       |   |        |   |       |
|     |      |             |         |           |       |   |        |   |       |
|     |      |             |         |           |       |   |        |   |       |
|     |      |             |         |           |       |   |        |   |       |
|     |      |             |         |           |       |   |        |   |       |
|     |      |             |         |           |       |   |        |   |       |
|     |      |             |         |           |       |   |        |   |       |
|     |      |             |         |           |       |   |        |   |       |
|     |      |             |         |           |       |   |        |   |       |
|     |      |             |         |           |       |   |        |   |       |
|     |      |             |         |           |       |   |        |   |       |
|     |      |             |         |           |       |   |        |   |       |
|     |      |             |         |           |       |   |        |   |       |

# ACCOUNTING LEDGER

PAGE.No.

**Account Name And Number :**

**Year :** _____     **Month :** _____

| No. | Date | Description | Account | Reference | Debit | − | Credit | + | Total |
|-----|------|-------------|---------|-----------|-------|---|--------|---|-------|
| | | | | | | | | | |
| | | | | | | | | | |
| | | | | | | | | | |
| | | | | | | | | | |
| | | | | | | | | | |
| | | | | | | | | | |
| | | | | | | | | | |
| | | | | | | | | | |
| | | | | | | | | | |
| | | | | | | | | | |
| | | | | | | | | | |
| | | | | | | | | | |
| | | | | | | | | | |
| | | | | | | | | | |
| | | | | | | | | | |
| | | | | | | | | | |
| | | | | | | | | | |
| | | | | | | | | | |
| | | | | | | | | | |
| | | | | | | | | | |
| | | | | | | | | | |
| | | | | | | | | | |
| | | | | | | | | | |
| | | | | | | | | | |
| | | | | | | | | | |
| | | | | | | | | | |
| | | | | | | | | | |
| | | | | | | | | | |

# ACCOUNTING LEDGER

**PAGE.No.**

**Account Name And Number :**

**Year :** _____        **Month :** _____

| No. | Date | Description | Account | Reference | Debit | − | Credit | + | Total |
|-----|------|-------------|---------|-----------|-------|---|--------|---|-------|
|     |      |             |         |           |       |   |        |   |       |
|     |      |             |         |           |       |   |        |   |       |
|     |      |             |         |           |       |   |        |   |       |
|     |      |             |         |           |       |   |        |   |       |
|     |      |             |         |           |       |   |        |   |       |
|     |      |             |         |           |       |   |        |   |       |
|     |      |             |         |           |       |   |        |   |       |
|     |      |             |         |           |       |   |        |   |       |
|     |      |             |         |           |       |   |        |   |       |
|     |      |             |         |           |       |   |        |   |       |
|     |      |             |         |           |       |   |        |   |       |
|     |      |             |         |           |       |   |        |   |       |
|     |      |             |         |           |       |   |        |   |       |
|     |      |             |         |           |       |   |        |   |       |
|     |      |             |         |           |       |   |        |   |       |
|     |      |             |         |           |       |   |        |   |       |
|     |      |             |         |           |       |   |        |   |       |
|     |      |             |         |           |       |   |        |   |       |
|     |      |             |         |           |       |   |        |   |       |
|     |      |             |         |           |       |   |        |   |       |
|     |      |             |         |           |       |   |        |   |       |
|     |      |             |         |           |       |   |        |   |       |
|     |      |             |         |           |       |   |        |   |       |
|     |      |             |         |           |       |   |        |   |       |
|     |      |             |         |           |       |   |        |   |       |
|     |      |             |         |           |       |   |        |   |       |
|     |      |             |         |           |       |   |        |   |       |
|     |      |             |         |           |       |   |        |   |       |

# ACCOUNTING LEDGER

**PAGE.No.**

**Account Name And Number :**

**Year : _____**                    **Month : _____**

| No. | Date | Description | Account | Reference | Debit | — | Credit | + | Total |
|-----|------|-------------|---------|-----------|-------|---|--------|---|-------|
| | | | | | | | | | |
| | | | | | | | | | |
| | | | | | | | | | |
| | | | | | | | | | |
| | | | | | | | | | |
| | | | | | | | | | |
| | | | | | | | | | |
| | | | | | | | | | |
| | | | | | | | | | |
| | | | | | | | | | |
| | | | | | | | | | |
| | | | | | | | | | |
| | | | | | | | | | |
| | | | | | | | | | |
| | | | | | | | | | |
| | | | | | | | | | |
| | | | | | | | | | |
| | | | | | | | | | |
| | | | | | | | | | |
| | | | | | | | | | |
| | | | | | | | | | |
| | | | | | | | | | |
| | | | | | | | | | |
| | | | | | | | | | |
| | | | | | | | | | |
| | | | | | | | | | |
| | | | | | | | | | |

# ACCOUNTING LEDGER

**PAGE.No.**

**Account Name And Number :**

**Year :** _____                                    **Month :** _____

| No. | Date | Description | Account | Reference | Debit | − | Credit | + | Total |
|-----|------|-------------|---------|-----------|-------|---|--------|---|-------|
|     |      |             |         |           |       |   |        |   |       |
|     |      |             |         |           |       |   |        |   |       |
|     |      |             |         |           |       |   |        |   |       |
|     |      |             |         |           |       |   |        |   |       |
|     |      |             |         |           |       |   |        |   |       |
|     |      |             |         |           |       |   |        |   |       |
|     |      |             |         |           |       |   |        |   |       |
|     |      |             |         |           |       |   |        |   |       |
|     |      |             |         |           |       |   |        |   |       |
|     |      |             |         |           |       |   |        |   |       |
|     |      |             |         |           |       |   |        |   |       |
|     |      |             |         |           |       |   |        |   |       |
|     |      |             |         |           |       |   |        |   |       |
|     |      |             |         |           |       |   |        |   |       |
|     |      |             |         |           |       |   |        |   |       |
|     |      |             |         |           |       |   |        |   |       |
|     |      |             |         |           |       |   |        |   |       |
|     |      |             |         |           |       |   |        |   |       |
|     |      |             |         |           |       |   |        |   |       |
|     |      |             |         |           |       |   |        |   |       |
|     |      |             |         |           |       |   |        |   |       |
|     |      |             |         |           |       |   |        |   |       |
|     |      |             |         |           |       |   |        |   |       |
|     |      |             |         |           |       |   |        |   |       |
|     |      |             |         |           |       |   |        |   |       |
|     |      |             |         |           |       |   |        |   |       |
|     |      |             |         |           |       |   |        |   |       |
|     |      |             |         |           |       |   |        |   |       |

# ACCOUNTING LEDGER

**PAGE.No.**

**Account Name And Number :**

**Year :** _____      **Month :** _____

| No. | Date | Description | Account | Reference | Debit | − | Credit | + | Total |
|-----|------|-------------|---------|-----------|-------|---|--------|---|-------|
|     |      |             |         |           |       |   |        |   |       |
|     |      |             |         |           |       |   |        |   |       |
|     |      |             |         |           |       |   |        |   |       |
|     |      |             |         |           |       |   |        |   |       |
|     |      |             |         |           |       |   |        |   |       |
|     |      |             |         |           |       |   |        |   |       |
|     |      |             |         |           |       |   |        |   |       |
|     |      |             |         |           |       |   |        |   |       |
|     |      |             |         |           |       |   |        |   |       |
|     |      |             |         |           |       |   |        |   |       |
|     |      |             |         |           |       |   |        |   |       |
|     |      |             |         |           |       |   |        |   |       |
|     |      |             |         |           |       |   |        |   |       |
|     |      |             |         |           |       |   |        |   |       |
|     |      |             |         |           |       |   |        |   |       |
|     |      |             |         |           |       |   |        |   |       |
|     |      |             |         |           |       |   |        |   |       |
|     |      |             |         |           |       |   |        |   |       |
|     |      |             |         |           |       |   |        |   |       |
|     |      |             |         |           |       |   |        |   |       |
|     |      |             |         |           |       |   |        |   |       |
|     |      |             |         |           |       |   |        |   |       |
|     |      |             |         |           |       |   |        |   |       |
|     |      |             |         |           |       |   |        |   |       |
|     |      |             |         |           |       |   |        |   |       |
|     |      |             |         |           |       |   |        |   |       |
|     |      |             |         |           |       |   |        |   |       |

# ACCOUNTING LEDGER

PAGE.No.

**Account Name And Number :**

**Year :** _____     **Month :** _____

| No. | Date | Description | Account | Reference | Debit | − | Credit | + | Total |
|-----|------|-------------|---------|-----------|-------|---|--------|---|-------|
| | | | | | | | | | |
| | | | | | | | | | |
| | | | | | | | | | |
| | | | | | | | | | |
| | | | | | | | | | |
| | | | | | | | | | |
| | | | | | | | | | |
| | | | | | | | | | |
| | | | | | | | | | |
| | | | | | | | | | |
| | | | | | | | | | |
| | | | | | | | | | |
| | | | | | | | | | |
| | | | | | | | | | |
| | | | | | | | | | |
| | | | | | | | | | |
| | | | | | | | | | |
| | | | | | | | | | |
| | | | | | | | | | |
| | | | | | | | | | |
| | | | | | | | | | |
| | | | | | | | | | |
| | | | | | | | | | |
| | | | | | | | | | |
| | | | | | | | | | |
| | | | | | | | | | |
| | | | | | | | | | |
| | | | | | | | | | |
| | | | | | | | | | |
| | | | | | | | | | |

# ACCOUNTING LEDGER

PAGE.No.

**Account Name And Number :**

**Year : _____**                                                    **Month : _____**

| No. | Date | Description | Account | Reference | Debit | − | Credit | + | Total |
|-----|------|-------------|---------|-----------|-------|---|--------|---|-------|
|     |      |             |         |           |       |   |        |   |       |
|     |      |             |         |           |       |   |        |   |       |
|     |      |             |         |           |       |   |        |   |       |
|     |      |             |         |           |       |   |        |   |       |
|     |      |             |         |           |       |   |        |   |       |
|     |      |             |         |           |       |   |        |   |       |
|     |      |             |         |           |       |   |        |   |       |
|     |      |             |         |           |       |   |        |   |       |
|     |      |             |         |           |       |   |        |   |       |
|     |      |             |         |           |       |   |        |   |       |
|     |      |             |         |           |       |   |        |   |       |
|     |      |             |         |           |       |   |        |   |       |
|     |      |             |         |           |       |   |        |   |       |
|     |      |             |         |           |       |   |        |   |       |
|     |      |             |         |           |       |   |        |   |       |
|     |      |             |         |           |       |   |        |   |       |
|     |      |             |         |           |       |   |        |   |       |
|     |      |             |         |           |       |   |        |   |       |
|     |      |             |         |           |       |   |        |   |       |
|     |      |             |         |           |       |   |        |   |       |
|     |      |             |         |           |       |   |        |   |       |
|     |      |             |         |           |       |   |        |   |       |
|     |      |             |         |           |       |   |        |   |       |
|     |      |             |         |           |       |   |        |   |       |
|     |      |             |         |           |       |   |        |   |       |
|     |      |             |         |           |       |   |        |   |       |
|     |      |             |         |           |       |   |        |   |       |

# ACCOUNTING LEDGER

PAGE.No.

**Account Name And Number :**

**Year : _____**                                    **Month : _____**

| No. | Date | Description | Account | Reference | Debit | − | Credit | + | Total |
|-----|------|-------------|---------|-----------|-------|---|--------|---|-------|
|     |      |             |         |           |       |   |        |   |       |
|     |      |             |         |           |       |   |        |   |       |
|     |      |             |         |           |       |   |        |   |       |
|     |      |             |         |           |       |   |        |   |       |
|     |      |             |         |           |       |   |        |   |       |
|     |      |             |         |           |       |   |        |   |       |
|     |      |             |         |           |       |   |        |   |       |
|     |      |             |         |           |       |   |        |   |       |
|     |      |             |         |           |       |   |        |   |       |
|     |      |             |         |           |       |   |        |   |       |
|     |      |             |         |           |       |   |        |   |       |
|     |      |             |         |           |       |   |        |   |       |
|     |      |             |         |           |       |   |        |   |       |
|     |      |             |         |           |       |   |        |   |       |
|     |      |             |         |           |       |   |        |   |       |
|     |      |             |         |           |       |   |        |   |       |
|     |      |             |         |           |       |   |        |   |       |
|     |      |             |         |           |       |   |        |   |       |
|     |      |             |         |           |       |   |        |   |       |
|     |      |             |         |           |       |   |        |   |       |
|     |      |             |         |           |       |   |        |   |       |
|     |      |             |         |           |       |   |        |   |       |
|     |      |             |         |           |       |   |        |   |       |
|     |      |             |         |           |       |   |        |   |       |
|     |      |             |         |           |       |   |        |   |       |
|     |      |             |         |           |       |   |        |   |       |
|     |      |             |         |           |       |   |        |   |       |
|     |      |             |         |           |       |   |        |   |       |
|     |      |             |         |           |       |   |        |   |       |

# ACCOUNTING LEDGER

**PAGE.No.**

**Account Name And Number :**

**Year : _____**                                          **Month : _____**

| No. | Date | Description | Account | Reference | Debit | − | Credit | + | Total |
|-----|------|-------------|---------|-----------|-------|---|--------|---|-------|
|     |      |             |         |           |       |   |        |   |       |
|     |      |             |         |           |       |   |        |   |       |
|     |      |             |         |           |       |   |        |   |       |
|     |      |             |         |           |       |   |        |   |       |
|     |      |             |         |           |       |   |        |   |       |
|     |      |             |         |           |       |   |        |   |       |
|     |      |             |         |           |       |   |        |   |       |
|     |      |             |         |           |       |   |        |   |       |
|     |      |             |         |           |       |   |        |   |       |
|     |      |             |         |           |       |   |        |   |       |
|     |      |             |         |           |       |   |        |   |       |
|     |      |             |         |           |       |   |        |   |       |
|     |      |             |         |           |       |   |        |   |       |
|     |      |             |         |           |       |   |        |   |       |
|     |      |             |         |           |       |   |        |   |       |
|     |      |             |         |           |       |   |        |   |       |
|     |      |             |         |           |       |   |        |   |       |
|     |      |             |         |           |       |   |        |   |       |
|     |      |             |         |           |       |   |        |   |       |
|     |      |             |         |           |       |   |        |   |       |
|     |      |             |         |           |       |   |        |   |       |
|     |      |             |         |           |       |   |        |   |       |
|     |      |             |         |           |       |   |        |   |       |
|     |      |             |         |           |       |   |        |   |       |
|     |      |             |         |           |       |   |        |   |       |
|     |      |             |         |           |       |   |        |   |       |

# ACCOUNTING LEDGER

**PAGE.No.**

**Account Name And Number :**

**Year :** _____

**Month :** _____

| No. | Date | Description | Account | Reference | Debit | − | Credit | + | Total |
|-----|------|-------------|---------|-----------|-------|---|--------|---|-------|
| | | | | | | | | | |
| | | | | | | | | | |
| | | | | | | | | | |
| | | | | | | | | | |
| | | | | | | | | | |
| | | | | | | | | | |
| | | | | | | | | | |
| | | | | | | | | | |
| | | | | | | | | | |
| | | | | | | | | | |
| | | | | | | | | | |
| | | | | | | | | | |
| | | | | | | | | | |
| | | | | | | | | | |
| | | | | | | | | | |
| | | | | | | | | | |
| | | | | | | | | | |
| | | | | | | | | | |
| | | | | | | | | | |
| | | | | | | | | | |
| | | | | | | | | | |
| | | | | | | | | | |
| | | | | | | | | | |
| | | | | | | | | | |
| | | | | | | | | | |
| | | | | | | | | | |
| | | | | | | | | | |
| | | | | | | | | | |
| | | | | | | | | | |

# ACCOUNTING LEDGER

PAGE.No.

**Account Name And Number :**

**Year :** _____  **Month :** _____

| No. | Date | Description | Account | Reference | Debit | − | Credit | + | Total |
|-----|------|-------------|---------|-----------|-------|---|--------|---|-------|
| | | | | | | | | | |
| | | | | | | | | | |
| | | | | | | | | | |
| | | | | | | | | | |
| | | | | | | | | | |
| | | | | | | | | | |
| | | | | | | | | | |
| | | | | | | | | | |
| | | | | | | | | | |
| | | | | | | | | | |
| | | | | | | | | | |
| | | | | | | | | | |
| | | | | | | | | | |
| | | | | | | | | | |
| | | | | | | | | | |
| | | | | | | | | | |
| | | | | | | | | | |
| | | | | | | | | | |
| | | | | | | | | | |
| | | | | | | | | | |
| | | | | | | | | | |
| | | | | | | | | | |
| | | | | | | | | | |
| | | | | | | | | | |
| | | | | | | | | | |
| | | | | | | | | | |
| | | | | | | | | | |

# ACCOUNTING LEDGER

**PAGE.No.**

**Account Name And Number :**

**Year : _____**                              **Month : _____**

| No. | Date | Description | Account | Reference | Debit | − | Credit | + | Total |
|-----|------|-------------|---------|-----------|-------|---|--------|---|-------|
|     |      |             |         |           |       |   |        |   |       |
|     |      |             |         |           |       |   |        |   |       |
|     |      |             |         |           |       |   |        |   |       |
|     |      |             |         |           |       |   |        |   |       |
|     |      |             |         |           |       |   |        |   |       |
|     |      |             |         |           |       |   |        |   |       |
|     |      |             |         |           |       |   |        |   |       |
|     |      |             |         |           |       |   |        |   |       |
|     |      |             |         |           |       |   |        |   |       |
|     |      |             |         |           |       |   |        |   |       |
|     |      |             |         |           |       |   |        |   |       |
|     |      |             |         |           |       |   |        |   |       |
|     |      |             |         |           |       |   |        |   |       |
|     |      |             |         |           |       |   |        |   |       |
|     |      |             |         |           |       |   |        |   |       |
|     |      |             |         |           |       |   |        |   |       |
|     |      |             |         |           |       |   |        |   |       |
|     |      |             |         |           |       |   |        |   |       |
|     |      |             |         |           |       |   |        |   |       |
|     |      |             |         |           |       |   |        |   |       |
|     |      |             |         |           |       |   |        |   |       |
|     |      |             |         |           |       |   |        |   |       |
|     |      |             |         |           |       |   |        |   |       |
|     |      |             |         |           |       |   |        |   |       |
|     |      |             |         |           |       |   |        |   |       |
|     |      |             |         |           |       |   |        |   |       |
|     |      |             |         |           |       |   |        |   |       |
|     |      |             |         |           |       |   |        |   |       |
|     |      |             |         |           |       |   |        |   |       |

# ACCOUNTING LEDGER

PAGE.No.

**Account Name And Number :**

**Year : _____**                                              **Month : _____**

| No. | Date | Description | Account | Reference | Debit | − | Credit | + | Total |
|-----|------|-------------|---------|-----------|-------|---|--------|---|-------|
|     |      |             |         |           |       |   |        |   |       |
|     |      |             |         |           |       |   |        |   |       |
|     |      |             |         |           |       |   |        |   |       |
|     |      |             |         |           |       |   |        |   |       |
|     |      |             |         |           |       |   |        |   |       |
|     |      |             |         |           |       |   |        |   |       |
|     |      |             |         |           |       |   |        |   |       |
|     |      |             |         |           |       |   |        |   |       |
|     |      |             |         |           |       |   |        |   |       |
|     |      |             |         |           |       |   |        |   |       |
|     |      |             |         |           |       |   |        |   |       |
|     |      |             |         |           |       |   |        |   |       |
|     |      |             |         |           |       |   |        |   |       |
|     |      |             |         |           |       |   |        |   |       |
|     |      |             |         |           |       |   |        |   |       |
|     |      |             |         |           |       |   |        |   |       |
|     |      |             |         |           |       |   |        |   |       |
|     |      |             |         |           |       |   |        |   |       |
|     |      |             |         |           |       |   |        |   |       |
|     |      |             |         |           |       |   |        |   |       |
|     |      |             |         |           |       |   |        |   |       |
|     |      |             |         |           |       |   |        |   |       |
|     |      |             |         |           |       |   |        |   |       |
|     |      |             |         |           |       |   |        |   |       |
|     |      |             |         |           |       |   |        |   |       |
|     |      |             |         |           |       |   |        |   |       |
|     |      |             |         |           |       |   |        |   |       |
|     |      |             |         |           |       |   |        |   |       |

# ACCOUNTING LEDGER

PAGE.No.

Account Name And Number :

Year : _____          Month : _____

| No. | Date | Description | Account | Reference | Debit | − | Credit | + | Total |
|-----|------|-------------|---------|-----------|-------|---|--------|---|-------|
|     |      |             |         |           |       |   |        |   |       |
|     |      |             |         |           |       |   |        |   |       |
|     |      |             |         |           |       |   |        |   |       |
|     |      |             |         |           |       |   |        |   |       |
|     |      |             |         |           |       |   |        |   |       |
|     |      |             |         |           |       |   |        |   |       |
|     |      |             |         |           |       |   |        |   |       |
|     |      |             |         |           |       |   |        |   |       |
|     |      |             |         |           |       |   |        |   |       |
|     |      |             |         |           |       |   |        |   |       |
|     |      |             |         |           |       |   |        |   |       |
|     |      |             |         |           |       |   |        |   |       |
|     |      |             |         |           |       |   |        |   |       |
|     |      |             |         |           |       |   |        |   |       |
|     |      |             |         |           |       |   |        |   |       |
|     |      |             |         |           |       |   |        |   |       |
|     |      |             |         |           |       |   |        |   |       |
|     |      |             |         |           |       |   |        |   |       |
|     |      |             |         |           |       |   |        |   |       |
|     |      |             |         |           |       |   |        |   |       |
|     |      |             |         |           |       |   |        |   |       |
|     |      |             |         |           |       |   |        |   |       |
|     |      |             |         |           |       |   |        |   |       |
|     |      |             |         |           |       |   |        |   |       |
|     |      |             |         |           |       |   |        |   |       |
|     |      |             |         |           |       |   |        |   |       |
|     |      |             |         |           |       |   |        |   |       |

# ACCOUNTING LEDGER

**PAGE.No.**

**Account Name And Number :**

**Year :** _____        **Month :** _____

| No. | Date | Description | Account | Reference | Debit | − | Credit | + | Total |
|-----|------|-------------|---------|-----------|-------|---|--------|---|-------|
|     |      |             |         |           |       |   |        |   |       |
|     |      |             |         |           |       |   |        |   |       |
|     |      |             |         |           |       |   |        |   |       |
|     |      |             |         |           |       |   |        |   |       |
|     |      |             |         |           |       |   |        |   |       |
|     |      |             |         |           |       |   |        |   |       |
|     |      |             |         |           |       |   |        |   |       |
|     |      |             |         |           |       |   |        |   |       |
|     |      |             |         |           |       |   |        |   |       |
|     |      |             |         |           |       |   |        |   |       |
|     |      |             |         |           |       |   |        |   |       |
|     |      |             |         |           |       |   |        |   |       |
|     |      |             |         |           |       |   |        |   |       |
|     |      |             |         |           |       |   |        |   |       |
|     |      |             |         |           |       |   |        |   |       |
|     |      |             |         |           |       |   |        |   |       |
|     |      |             |         |           |       |   |        |   |       |
|     |      |             |         |           |       |   |        |   |       |
|     |      |             |         |           |       |   |        |   |       |
|     |      |             |         |           |       |   |        |   |       |
|     |      |             |         |           |       |   |        |   |       |
|     |      |             |         |           |       |   |        |   |       |
|     |      |             |         |           |       |   |        |   |       |
|     |      |             |         |           |       |   |        |   |       |
|     |      |             |         |           |       |   |        |   |       |
|     |      |             |         |           |       |   |        |   |       |
|     |      |             |         |           |       |   |        |   |       |
|     |      |             |         |           |       |   |        |   |       |

# ACCOUNTING LEDGER

**PAGE.No.**

**Account Name And Number :**

**Year : _____**　　　　　　　　　　　　**Month : _____**

| No. | Date | Description | Account | Reference | Debit | − | Credit | + | Total |
|-----|------|-------------|---------|-----------|-------|---|--------|---|-------|
|  |  |  |  |  |  |  |  |  |  |
|  |  |  |  |  |  |  |  |  |  |
|  |  |  |  |  |  |  |  |  |  |
|  |  |  |  |  |  |  |  |  |  |
|  |  |  |  |  |  |  |  |  |  |
|  |  |  |  |  |  |  |  |  |  |
|  |  |  |  |  |  |  |  |  |  |
|  |  |  |  |  |  |  |  |  |  |
|  |  |  |  |  |  |  |  |  |  |
|  |  |  |  |  |  |  |  |  |  |
|  |  |  |  |  |  |  |  |  |  |
|  |  |  |  |  |  |  |  |  |  |
|  |  |  |  |  |  |  |  |  |  |
|  |  |  |  |  |  |  |  |  |  |
|  |  |  |  |  |  |  |  |  |  |
|  |  |  |  |  |  |  |  |  |  |
|  |  |  |  |  |  |  |  |  |  |
|  |  |  |  |  |  |  |  |  |  |
|  |  |  |  |  |  |  |  |  |  |
|  |  |  |  |  |  |  |  |  |  |
|  |  |  |  |  |  |  |  |  |  |
|  |  |  |  |  |  |  |  |  |  |
|  |  |  |  |  |  |  |  |  |  |
|  |  |  |  |  |  |  |  |  |  |
|  |  |  |  |  |  |  |  |  |  |

# ACCOUNTING LEDGER

PAGE.No.

**Account Name And Number :**

**Year : _____**                                      **Month : _____**

| No. | Date | Description | Account | Reference | Debit | − | Credit | + | Total |
|-----|------|-------------|---------|-----------|-------|---|--------|---|-------|
|  |  |  |  |  |  |  |  |  |  |
|  |  |  |  |  |  |  |  |  |  |
|  |  |  |  |  |  |  |  |  |  |
|  |  |  |  |  |  |  |  |  |  |
|  |  |  |  |  |  |  |  |  |  |
|  |  |  |  |  |  |  |  |  |  |
|  |  |  |  |  |  |  |  |  |  |
|  |  |  |  |  |  |  |  |  |  |
|  |  |  |  |  |  |  |  |  |  |
|  |  |  |  |  |  |  |  |  |  |
|  |  |  |  |  |  |  |  |  |  |
|  |  |  |  |  |  |  |  |  |  |
|  |  |  |  |  |  |  |  |  |  |
|  |  |  |  |  |  |  |  |  |  |
|  |  |  |  |  |  |  |  |  |  |
|  |  |  |  |  |  |  |  |  |  |
|  |  |  |  |  |  |  |  |  |  |
|  |  |  |  |  |  |  |  |  |  |
|  |  |  |  |  |  |  |  |  |  |
|  |  |  |  |  |  |  |  |  |  |
|  |  |  |  |  |  |  |  |  |  |
|  |  |  |  |  |  |  |  |  |  |
|  |  |  |  |  |  |  |  |  |  |
|  |  |  |  |  |  |  |  |  |  |
|  |  |  |  |  |  |  |  |  |  |
|  |  |  |  |  |  |  |  |  |  |
|  |  |  |  |  |  |  |  |  |  |
|  |  |  |  |  |  |  |  |  |  |
|  |  |  |  |  |  |  |  |  |  |

# ACCOUNTING LEDGER

PAGE.No.

**Account Name And Number :**

**Year :** _____                                                **Month :** _____

| No. | Date | Description | Account | Reference | Debit | − | Credit | + | Total |
|-----|------|-------------|---------|-----------|-------|---|--------|---|-------|
| | | | | | | | | | |
| | | | | | | | | | |
| | | | | | | | | | |
| | | | | | | | | | |
| | | | | | | | | | |
| | | | | | | | | | |
| | | | | | | | | | |
| | | | | | | | | | |
| | | | | | | | | | |
| | | | | | | | | | |
| | | | | | | | | | |
| | | | | | | | | | |
| | | | | | | | | | |
| | | | | | | | | | |
| | | | | | | | | | |
| | | | | | | | | | |
| | | | | | | | | | |
| | | | | | | | | | |
| | | | | | | | | | |
| | | | | | | | | | |
| | | | | | | | | | |
| | | | | | | | | | |
| | | | | | | | | | |
| | | | | | | | | | |
| | | | | | | | | | |
| | | | | | | | | | |
| | | | | | | | | | |

# ACCOUNTING LEDGER

PAGE.No.

Account Name And Number :

Year : _____                                    Month : _____

| No. | Date | Description | Account | Reference | Debit | – | Credit | + | Total |
|-----|------|-------------|---------|-----------|-------|---|--------|---|-------|
|     |      |             |         |           |       |   |        |   |       |
|     |      |             |         |           |       |   |        |   |       |
|     |      |             |         |           |       |   |        |   |       |
|     |      |             |         |           |       |   |        |   |       |
|     |      |             |         |           |       |   |        |   |       |
|     |      |             |         |           |       |   |        |   |       |
|     |      |             |         |           |       |   |        |   |       |
|     |      |             |         |           |       |   |        |   |       |
|     |      |             |         |           |       |   |        |   |       |
|     |      |             |         |           |       |   |        |   |       |
|     |      |             |         |           |       |   |        |   |       |
|     |      |             |         |           |       |   |        |   |       |
|     |      |             |         |           |       |   |        |   |       |
|     |      |             |         |           |       |   |        |   |       |
|     |      |             |         |           |       |   |        |   |       |
|     |      |             |         |           |       |   |        |   |       |
|     |      |             |         |           |       |   |        |   |       |
|     |      |             |         |           |       |   |        |   |       |
|     |      |             |         |           |       |   |        |   |       |
|     |      |             |         |           |       |   |        |   |       |
|     |      |             |         |           |       |   |        |   |       |
|     |      |             |         |           |       |   |        |   |       |
|     |      |             |         |           |       |   |        |   |       |
|     |      |             |         |           |       |   |        |   |       |
|     |      |             |         |           |       |   |        |   |       |
|     |      |             |         |           |       |   |        |   |       |

# ACCOUNTING LEDGER

**PAGE.No.**

**Account Name And Number :**

**Year :** _____          **Month :** _____

| No. | Date | Description | Account | Reference | Debit | − | Credit | + | Total |
|-----|------|-------------|---------|-----------|-------|---|--------|---|-------|
|     |      |             |         |           |       |   |        |   |       |
|     |      |             |         |           |       |   |        |   |       |
|     |      |             |         |           |       |   |        |   |       |
|     |      |             |         |           |       |   |        |   |       |
|     |      |             |         |           |       |   |        |   |       |
|     |      |             |         |           |       |   |        |   |       |
|     |      |             |         |           |       |   |        |   |       |
|     |      |             |         |           |       |   |        |   |       |
|     |      |             |         |           |       |   |        |   |       |
|     |      |             |         |           |       |   |        |   |       |
|     |      |             |         |           |       |   |        |   |       |
|     |      |             |         |           |       |   |        |   |       |
|     |      |             |         |           |       |   |        |   |       |
|     |      |             |         |           |       |   |        |   |       |
|     |      |             |         |           |       |   |        |   |       |
|     |      |             |         |           |       |   |        |   |       |
|     |      |             |         |           |       |   |        |   |       |
|     |      |             |         |           |       |   |        |   |       |
|     |      |             |         |           |       |   |        |   |       |
|     |      |             |         |           |       |   |        |   |       |
|     |      |             |         |           |       |   |        |   |       |
|     |      |             |         |           |       |   |        |   |       |
|     |      |             |         |           |       |   |        |   |       |
|     |      |             |         |           |       |   |        |   |       |
|     |      |             |         |           |       |   |        |   |       |
|     |      |             |         |           |       |   |        |   |       |
|     |      |             |         |           |       |   |        |   |       |
|     |      |             |         |           |       |   |        |   |       |

# ACCOUNTING LEDGER

PAGE.No.

**Account Name And Number :**

**Year : _____**                                    **Month : _____**

| No. | Date | Description | Account | Reference | Debit | − | Credit | + | Total |
|-----|------|-------------|---------|-----------|-------|---|--------|---|-------|
|     |      |             |         |           |       |   |        |   |       |
|     |      |             |         |           |       |   |        |   |       |
|     |      |             |         |           |       |   |        |   |       |
|     |      |             |         |           |       |   |        |   |       |
|     |      |             |         |           |       |   |        |   |       |
|     |      |             |         |           |       |   |        |   |       |
|     |      |             |         |           |       |   |        |   |       |
|     |      |             |         |           |       |   |        |   |       |
|     |      |             |         |           |       |   |        |   |       |
|     |      |             |         |           |       |   |        |   |       |
|     |      |             |         |           |       |   |        |   |       |
|     |      |             |         |           |       |   |        |   |       |
|     |      |             |         |           |       |   |        |   |       |
|     |      |             |         |           |       |   |        |   |       |
|     |      |             |         |           |       |   |        |   |       |
|     |      |             |         |           |       |   |        |   |       |
|     |      |             |         |           |       |   |        |   |       |
|     |      |             |         |           |       |   |        |   |       |
|     |      |             |         |           |       |   |        |   |       |
|     |      |             |         |           |       |   |        |   |       |
|     |      |             |         |           |       |   |        |   |       |
|     |      |             |         |           |       |   |        |   |       |
|     |      |             |         |           |       |   |        |   |       |
|     |      |             |         |           |       |   |        |   |       |
|     |      |             |         |           |       |   |        |   |       |
|     |      |             |         |           |       |   |        |   |       |

# ACCOUNTING LEDGER

**PAGE.No.**

**Account Name And Number :**

**Year :** ____                                    **Month :** ____

| No. | Date | Description | Account | Reference | Debit | − | Credit | + | Total |
|-----|------|-------------|---------|-----------|-------|---|--------|---|-------|
|     |      |             |         |           |       |   |        |   |       |
|     |      |             |         |           |       |   |        |   |       |
|     |      |             |         |           |       |   |        |   |       |
|     |      |             |         |           |       |   |        |   |       |
|     |      |             |         |           |       |   |        |   |       |
|     |      |             |         |           |       |   |        |   |       |
|     |      |             |         |           |       |   |        |   |       |
|     |      |             |         |           |       |   |        |   |       |
|     |      |             |         |           |       |   |        |   |       |
|     |      |             |         |           |       |   |        |   |       |
|     |      |             |         |           |       |   |        |   |       |
|     |      |             |         |           |       |   |        |   |       |
|     |      |             |         |           |       |   |        |   |       |
|     |      |             |         |           |       |   |        |   |       |
|     |      |             |         |           |       |   |        |   |       |
|     |      |             |         |           |       |   |        |   |       |
|     |      |             |         |           |       |   |        |   |       |
|     |      |             |         |           |       |   |        |   |       |
|     |      |             |         |           |       |   |        |   |       |
|     |      |             |         |           |       |   |        |   |       |
|     |      |             |         |           |       |   |        |   |       |
|     |      |             |         |           |       |   |        |   |       |
|     |      |             |         |           |       |   |        |   |       |
|     |      |             |         |           |       |   |        |   |       |
|     |      |             |         |           |       |   |        |   |       |
|     |      |             |         |           |       |   |        |   |       |
|     |      |             |         |           |       |   |        |   |       |

# ACCOUNTING LEDGER

**PAGE.No.**

**Account Name And Number :**

**Year :** _____          **Month :** _____

| No. | Date | Description | Account | Reference | Debit | − | Credit | + | Total |
|-----|------|-------------|---------|-----------|-------|---|--------|---|-------|
|     |      |             |         |           |       |   |        |   |       |
|     |      |             |         |           |       |   |        |   |       |
|     |      |             |         |           |       |   |        |   |       |
|     |      |             |         |           |       |   |        |   |       |
|     |      |             |         |           |       |   |        |   |       |
|     |      |             |         |           |       |   |        |   |       |
|     |      |             |         |           |       |   |        |   |       |
|     |      |             |         |           |       |   |        |   |       |
|     |      |             |         |           |       |   |        |   |       |
|     |      |             |         |           |       |   |        |   |       |
|     |      |             |         |           |       |   |        |   |       |
|     |      |             |         |           |       |   |        |   |       |
|     |      |             |         |           |       |   |        |   |       |
|     |      |             |         |           |       |   |        |   |       |
|     |      |             |         |           |       |   |        |   |       |
|     |      |             |         |           |       |   |        |   |       |
|     |      |             |         |           |       |   |        |   |       |
|     |      |             |         |           |       |   |        |   |       |
|     |      |             |         |           |       |   |        |   |       |
|     |      |             |         |           |       |   |        |   |       |
|     |      |             |         |           |       |   |        |   |       |
|     |      |             |         |           |       |   |        |   |       |
|     |      |             |         |           |       |   |        |   |       |
|     |      |             |         |           |       |   |        |   |       |
|     |      |             |         |           |       |   |        |   |       |

# ACCOUNTING LEDGER

**PAGE.No.**

**Account Name And Number :**

**Year :** _____          **Month :** _____

| No. | Date | Description | Account | Reference | Debit | — | Credit | + | Total |
|-----|------|-------------|---------|-----------|-------|---|--------|---|-------|
|     |      |             |         |           |       |   |        |   |       |
|     |      |             |         |           |       |   |        |   |       |
|     |      |             |         |           |       |   |        |   |       |
|     |      |             |         |           |       |   |        |   |       |
|     |      |             |         |           |       |   |        |   |       |
|     |      |             |         |           |       |   |        |   |       |
|     |      |             |         |           |       |   |        |   |       |
|     |      |             |         |           |       |   |        |   |       |
|     |      |             |         |           |       |   |        |   |       |
|     |      |             |         |           |       |   |        |   |       |
|     |      |             |         |           |       |   |        |   |       |
|     |      |             |         |           |       |   |        |   |       |
|     |      |             |         |           |       |   |        |   |       |
|     |      |             |         |           |       |   |        |   |       |
|     |      |             |         |           |       |   |        |   |       |
|     |      |             |         |           |       |   |        |   |       |
|     |      |             |         |           |       |   |        |   |       |
|     |      |             |         |           |       |   |        |   |       |
|     |      |             |         |           |       |   |        |   |       |
|     |      |             |         |           |       |   |        |   |       |
|     |      |             |         |           |       |   |        |   |       |
|     |      |             |         |           |       |   |        |   |       |
|     |      |             |         |           |       |   |        |   |       |
|     |      |             |         |           |       |   |        |   |       |
|     |      |             |         |           |       |   |        |   |       |
|     |      |             |         |           |       |   |        |   |       |
|     |      |             |         |           |       |   |        |   |       |
|     |      |             |         |           |       |   |        |   |       |
|     |      |             |         |           |       |   |        |   |       |
|     |      |             |         |           |       |   |        |   |       |
|     |      |             |         |           |       |   |        |   |       |

# ACCOUNTING LEDGER

PAGE.No.

**Account Name And Number :**

Year : _____                                          Month : _____

| No. | Date | Description | Account | Reference | Debit | − | Credit | + | Total |
|-----|------|-------------|---------|-----------|-------|---|--------|---|-------|
|     |      |             |         |           |       |   |        |   |       |
|     |      |             |         |           |       |   |        |   |       |
|     |      |             |         |           |       |   |        |   |       |
|     |      |             |         |           |       |   |        |   |       |
|     |      |             |         |           |       |   |        |   |       |
|     |      |             |         |           |       |   |        |   |       |
|     |      |             |         |           |       |   |        |   |       |
|     |      |             |         |           |       |   |        |   |       |
|     |      |             |         |           |       |   |        |   |       |
|     |      |             |         |           |       |   |        |   |       |
|     |      |             |         |           |       |   |        |   |       |
|     |      |             |         |           |       |   |        |   |       |
|     |      |             |         |           |       |   |        |   |       |
|     |      |             |         |           |       |   |        |   |       |
|     |      |             |         |           |       |   |        |   |       |
|     |      |             |         |           |       |   |        |   |       |
|     |      |             |         |           |       |   |        |   |       |
|     |      |             |         |           |       |   |        |   |       |
|     |      |             |         |           |       |   |        |   |       |
|     |      |             |         |           |       |   |        |   |       |
|     |      |             |         |           |       |   |        |   |       |
|     |      |             |         |           |       |   |        |   |       |
|     |      |             |         |           |       |   |        |   |       |
|     |      |             |         |           |       |   |        |   |       |
|     |      |             |         |           |       |   |        |   |       |
|     |      |             |         |           |       |   |        |   |       |
|     |      |             |         |           |       |   |        |   |       |
|     |      |             |         |           |       |   |        |   |       |
|     |      |             |         |           |       |   |        |   |       |

# ACCOUNTING LEDGER

**PAGE.No.**

**Account Name And Number :**

**Year : ____**

**Month : ____**

| No. | Date | Description | Account | Reference | Debit | − | Credit | + | Total |
|-----|------|-------------|---------|-----------|-------|---|--------|---|-------|
|     |      |             |         |           |       |   |        |   |       |
|     |      |             |         |           |       |   |        |   |       |
|     |      |             |         |           |       |   |        |   |       |
|     |      |             |         |           |       |   |        |   |       |
|     |      |             |         |           |       |   |        |   |       |
|     |      |             |         |           |       |   |        |   |       |
|     |      |             |         |           |       |   |        |   |       |
|     |      |             |         |           |       |   |        |   |       |
|     |      |             |         |           |       |   |        |   |       |
|     |      |             |         |           |       |   |        |   |       |
|     |      |             |         |           |       |   |        |   |       |
|     |      |             |         |           |       |   |        |   |       |
|     |      |             |         |           |       |   |        |   |       |
|     |      |             |         |           |       |   |        |   |       |
|     |      |             |         |           |       |   |        |   |       |
|     |      |             |         |           |       |   |        |   |       |
|     |      |             |         |           |       |   |        |   |       |
|     |      |             |         |           |       |   |        |   |       |
|     |      |             |         |           |       |   |        |   |       |
|     |      |             |         |           |       |   |        |   |       |
|     |      |             |         |           |       |   |        |   |       |
|     |      |             |         |           |       |   |        |   |       |
|     |      |             |         |           |       |   |        |   |       |
|     |      |             |         |           |       |   |        |   |       |
|     |      |             |         |           |       |   |        |   |       |
|     |      |             |         |           |       |   |        |   |       |
|     |      |             |         |           |       |   |        |   |       |
|     |      |             |         |           |       |   |        |   |       |

# ACCOUNTING LEDGER

**PAGE.No.**

**Account Name And Number :**

**Year : _____**          **Month : _____**

| No. | Date | Description | Account | Reference | Debit | − | Credit | + | Total |
|-----|------|-------------|---------|-----------|-------|---|--------|---|-------|
|     |      |             |         |           |       |   |        |   |       |
|     |      |             |         |           |       |   |        |   |       |
|     |      |             |         |           |       |   |        |   |       |
|     |      |             |         |           |       |   |        |   |       |
|     |      |             |         |           |       |   |        |   |       |
|     |      |             |         |           |       |   |        |   |       |
|     |      |             |         |           |       |   |        |   |       |
|     |      |             |         |           |       |   |        |   |       |
|     |      |             |         |           |       |   |        |   |       |
|     |      |             |         |           |       |   |        |   |       |
|     |      |             |         |           |       |   |        |   |       |
|     |      |             |         |           |       |   |        |   |       |
|     |      |             |         |           |       |   |        |   |       |
|     |      |             |         |           |       |   |        |   |       |
|     |      |             |         |           |       |   |        |   |       |
|     |      |             |         |           |       |   |        |   |       |
|     |      |             |         |           |       |   |        |   |       |
|     |      |             |         |           |       |   |        |   |       |
|     |      |             |         |           |       |   |        |   |       |
|     |      |             |         |           |       |   |        |   |       |
|     |      |             |         |           |       |   |        |   |       |
|     |      |             |         |           |       |   |        |   |       |
|     |      |             |         |           |       |   |        |   |       |
|     |      |             |         |           |       |   |        |   |       |
|     |      |             |         |           |       |   |        |   |       |
|     |      |             |         |           |       |   |        |   |       |
|     |      |             |         |           |       |   |        |   |       |
|     |      |             |         |           |       |   |        |   |       |

# ACCOUNTING LEDGER

**PAGE.No.**

**Account Name And Number :**

**Year :** _____          **Month :** _____

| No. | Date | Description | Account | Reference | Debit | − | Credit | + | Total |
|-----|------|-------------|---------|-----------|-------|---|--------|---|-------|
|     |      |             |         |           |       |   |        |   |       |
|     |      |             |         |           |       |   |        |   |       |
|     |      |             |         |           |       |   |        |   |       |
|     |      |             |         |           |       |   |        |   |       |
|     |      |             |         |           |       |   |        |   |       |
|     |      |             |         |           |       |   |        |   |       |
|     |      |             |         |           |       |   |        |   |       |
|     |      |             |         |           |       |   |        |   |       |
|     |      |             |         |           |       |   |        |   |       |
|     |      |             |         |           |       |   |        |   |       |
|     |      |             |         |           |       |   |        |   |       |
|     |      |             |         |           |       |   |        |   |       |
|     |      |             |         |           |       |   |        |   |       |
|     |      |             |         |           |       |   |        |   |       |
|     |      |             |         |           |       |   |        |   |       |
|     |      |             |         |           |       |   |        |   |       |
|     |      |             |         |           |       |   |        |   |       |
|     |      |             |         |           |       |   |        |   |       |
|     |      |             |         |           |       |   |        |   |       |
|     |      |             |         |           |       |   |        |   |       |
|     |      |             |         |           |       |   |        |   |       |
|     |      |             |         |           |       |   |        |   |       |
|     |      |             |         |           |       |   |        |   |       |
|     |      |             |         |           |       |   |        |   |       |
|     |      |             |         |           |       |   |        |   |       |
|     |      |             |         |           |       |   |        |   |       |
|     |      |             |         |           |       |   |        |   |       |
|     |      |             |         |           |       |   |        |   |       |

# ACCOUNTING LEDGER

PAGE.No.

Account Name And Number :

Year : _____                                    Month : _____

| No. | Date | Description | Account | Reference | Debit | − | Credit | + | Total |
|-----|------|-------------|---------|-----------|-------|---|--------|---|-------|
|     |      |             |         |           |       |   |        |   |       |
|     |      |             |         |           |       |   |        |   |       |
|     |      |             |         |           |       |   |        |   |       |
|     |      |             |         |           |       |   |        |   |       |
|     |      |             |         |           |       |   |        |   |       |
|     |      |             |         |           |       |   |        |   |       |
|     |      |             |         |           |       |   |        |   |       |
|     |      |             |         |           |       |   |        |   |       |
|     |      |             |         |           |       |   |        |   |       |
|     |      |             |         |           |       |   |        |   |       |
|     |      |             |         |           |       |   |        |   |       |
|     |      |             |         |           |       |   |        |   |       |
|     |      |             |         |           |       |   |        |   |       |
|     |      |             |         |           |       |   |        |   |       |
|     |      |             |         |           |       |   |        |   |       |
|     |      |             |         |           |       |   |        |   |       |
|     |      |             |         |           |       |   |        |   |       |
|     |      |             |         |           |       |   |        |   |       |
|     |      |             |         |           |       |   |        |   |       |
|     |      |             |         |           |       |   |        |   |       |
|     |      |             |         |           |       |   |        |   |       |
|     |      |             |         |           |       |   |        |   |       |
|     |      |             |         |           |       |   |        |   |       |
|     |      |             |         |           |       |   |        |   |       |
|     |      |             |         |           |       |   |        |   |       |
|     |      |             |         |           |       |   |        |   |       |
|     |      |             |         |           |       |   |        |   |       |
|     |      |             |         |           |       |   |        |   |       |

# ACCOUNTING LEDGER

**PAGE.No.**

**Account Name And Number :**

**Year : _____**                                           **Month : _____**

| No. | Date | Description | Account | Reference | Debit | − | Credit | + | Total |
|-----|------|-------------|---------|-----------|-------|---|--------|---|-------|
|     |      |             |         |           |       |   |        |   |       |
|     |      |             |         |           |       |   |        |   |       |
|     |      |             |         |           |       |   |        |   |       |
|     |      |             |         |           |       |   |        |   |       |
|     |      |             |         |           |       |   |        |   |       |
|     |      |             |         |           |       |   |        |   |       |
|     |      |             |         |           |       |   |        |   |       |
|     |      |             |         |           |       |   |        |   |       |
|     |      |             |         |           |       |   |        |   |       |
|     |      |             |         |           |       |   |        |   |       |
|     |      |             |         |           |       |   |        |   |       |
|     |      |             |         |           |       |   |        |   |       |
|     |      |             |         |           |       |   |        |   |       |
|     |      |             |         |           |       |   |        |   |       |
|     |      |             |         |           |       |   |        |   |       |
|     |      |             |         |           |       |   |        |   |       |
|     |      |             |         |           |       |   |        |   |       |
|     |      |             |         |           |       |   |        |   |       |
|     |      |             |         |           |       |   |        |   |       |
|     |      |             |         |           |       |   |        |   |       |
|     |      |             |         |           |       |   |        |   |       |
|     |      |             |         |           |       |   |        |   |       |
|     |      |             |         |           |       |   |        |   |       |
|     |      |             |         |           |       |   |        |   |       |
|     |      |             |         |           |       |   |        |   |       |
|     |      |             |         |           |       |   |        |   |       |

# ACCOUNTING LEDGER

**PAGE.No.**

**Account Name And Number :**

**Year : _____**                                    **Month : _____**

| No. | Date | Description | Account | Reference | Debit | − | Credit | + | Total |
|-----|------|-------------|---------|-----------|-------|---|--------|---|-------|
|     |      |             |         |           |       |   |        |   |       |
|     |      |             |         |           |       |   |        |   |       |
|     |      |             |         |           |       |   |        |   |       |
|     |      |             |         |           |       |   |        |   |       |
|     |      |             |         |           |       |   |        |   |       |
|     |      |             |         |           |       |   |        |   |       |
|     |      |             |         |           |       |   |        |   |       |
|     |      |             |         |           |       |   |        |   |       |
|     |      |             |         |           |       |   |        |   |       |
|     |      |             |         |           |       |   |        |   |       |
|     |      |             |         |           |       |   |        |   |       |
|     |      |             |         |           |       |   |        |   |       |
|     |      |             |         |           |       |   |        |   |       |
|     |      |             |         |           |       |   |        |   |       |
|     |      |             |         |           |       |   |        |   |       |
|     |      |             |         |           |       |   |        |   |       |
|     |      |             |         |           |       |   |        |   |       |
|     |      |             |         |           |       |   |        |   |       |
|     |      |             |         |           |       |   |        |   |       |
|     |      |             |         |           |       |   |        |   |       |
|     |      |             |         |           |       |   |        |   |       |
|     |      |             |         |           |       |   |        |   |       |
|     |      |             |         |           |       |   |        |   |       |
|     |      |             |         |           |       |   |        |   |       |
|     |      |             |         |           |       |   |        |   |       |
|     |      |             |         |           |       |   |        |   |       |
|     |      |             |         |           |       |   |        |   |       |

# ACCOUNTING LEDGER

**PAGE.No.**

**Account Name And Number :**

**Year : _____**   **Month : _____**

| No. | Date | Description | Account | Reference | Debit | − | Credit | + | Total |
|-----|------|-------------|---------|-----------|-------|---|--------|---|-------|
|     |      |             |         |           |       |   |        |   |       |
|     |      |             |         |           |       |   |        |   |       |
|     |      |             |         |           |       |   |        |   |       |
|     |      |             |         |           |       |   |        |   |       |
|     |      |             |         |           |       |   |        |   |       |
|     |      |             |         |           |       |   |        |   |       |
|     |      |             |         |           |       |   |        |   |       |
|     |      |             |         |           |       |   |        |   |       |
|     |      |             |         |           |       |   |        |   |       |
|     |      |             |         |           |       |   |        |   |       |
|     |      |             |         |           |       |   |        |   |       |
|     |      |             |         |           |       |   |        |   |       |
|     |      |             |         |           |       |   |        |   |       |
|     |      |             |         |           |       |   |        |   |       |
|     |      |             |         |           |       |   |        |   |       |
|     |      |             |         |           |       |   |        |   |       |
|     |      |             |         |           |       |   |        |   |       |
|     |      |             |         |           |       |   |        |   |       |
|     |      |             |         |           |       |   |        |   |       |
|     |      |             |         |           |       |   |        |   |       |
|     |      |             |         |           |       |   |        |   |       |
|     |      |             |         |           |       |   |        |   |       |
|     |      |             |         |           |       |   |        |   |       |
|     |      |             |         |           |       |   |        |   |       |
|     |      |             |         |           |       |   |        |   |       |
|     |      |             |         |           |       |   |        |   |       |
|     |      |             |         |           |       |   |        |   |       |
|     |      |             |         |           |       |   |        |   |       |
|     |      |             |         |           |       |   |        |   |       |
|     |      |             |         |           |       |   |        |   |       |

# ACCOUNTING LEDGER

**PAGE.No.**

**Account Name And Number :**

**Year :** \_\_\_\_

**Month :** \_\_\_\_

| No. | Date | Description | Account | Reference | Debit | − | Credit | + | Total |
|-----|------|-------------|---------|-----------|-------|---|--------|---|-------|
|     |      |             |         |           |       |   |        |   |       |
|     |      |             |         |           |       |   |        |   |       |
|     |      |             |         |           |       |   |        |   |       |
|     |      |             |         |           |       |   |        |   |       |
|     |      |             |         |           |       |   |        |   |       |
|     |      |             |         |           |       |   |        |   |       |
|     |      |             |         |           |       |   |        |   |       |
|     |      |             |         |           |       |   |        |   |       |
|     |      |             |         |           |       |   |        |   |       |
|     |      |             |         |           |       |   |        |   |       |
|     |      |             |         |           |       |   |        |   |       |
|     |      |             |         |           |       |   |        |   |       |
|     |      |             |         |           |       |   |        |   |       |
|     |      |             |         |           |       |   |        |   |       |
|     |      |             |         |           |       |   |        |   |       |
|     |      |             |         |           |       |   |        |   |       |
|     |      |             |         |           |       |   |        |   |       |
|     |      |             |         |           |       |   |        |   |       |
|     |      |             |         |           |       |   |        |   |       |
|     |      |             |         |           |       |   |        |   |       |
|     |      |             |         |           |       |   |        |   |       |
|     |      |             |         |           |       |   |        |   |       |
|     |      |             |         |           |       |   |        |   |       |
|     |      |             |         |           |       |   |        |   |       |
|     |      |             |         |           |       |   |        |   |       |
|     |      |             |         |           |       |   |        |   |       |
|     |      |             |         |           |       |   |        |   |       |

# ACCOUNTING LEDGER

PAGE.No.

Account Name And Number :

Year : _____       Month : _____

| No. | Date | Description | Account | Reference | Debit | — | Credit | + | Total |
|-----|------|-------------|---------|-----------|-------|---|--------|---|-------|
|     |      |             |         |           |       |   |        |   |       |
|     |      |             |         |           |       |   |        |   |       |
|     |      |             |         |           |       |   |        |   |       |
|     |      |             |         |           |       |   |        |   |       |
|     |      |             |         |           |       |   |        |   |       |
|     |      |             |         |           |       |   |        |   |       |
|     |      |             |         |           |       |   |        |   |       |
|     |      |             |         |           |       |   |        |   |       |
|     |      |             |         |           |       |   |        |   |       |
|     |      |             |         |           |       |   |        |   |       |
|     |      |             |         |           |       |   |        |   |       |
|     |      |             |         |           |       |   |        |   |       |
|     |      |             |         |           |       |   |        |   |       |
|     |      |             |         |           |       |   |        |   |       |
|     |      |             |         |           |       |   |        |   |       |
|     |      |             |         |           |       |   |        |   |       |
|     |      |             |         |           |       |   |        |   |       |
|     |      |             |         |           |       |   |        |   |       |
|     |      |             |         |           |       |   |        |   |       |
|     |      |             |         |           |       |   |        |   |       |
|     |      |             |         |           |       |   |        |   |       |
|     |      |             |         |           |       |   |        |   |       |
|     |      |             |         |           |       |   |        |   |       |
|     |      |             |         |           |       |   |        |   |       |
|     |      |             |         |           |       |   |        |   |       |
|     |      |             |         |           |       |   |        |   |       |
|     |      |             |         |           |       |   |        |   |       |
|     |      |             |         |           |       |   |        |   |       |

# ACCOUNTING LEDGER

**PAGE.No.**

**Account Name And Number :**

**Year : _____**                    **Month : _____**

| No. | Date | Description | Account | Reference | Debit | − | Credit | + | Total |
|-----|------|-------------|---------|-----------|-------|---|--------|---|-------|
|     |      |             |         |           |       |   |        |   |       |
|     |      |             |         |           |       |   |        |   |       |
|     |      |             |         |           |       |   |        |   |       |
|     |      |             |         |           |       |   |        |   |       |
|     |      |             |         |           |       |   |        |   |       |
|     |      |             |         |           |       |   |        |   |       |
|     |      |             |         |           |       |   |        |   |       |
|     |      |             |         |           |       |   |        |   |       |
|     |      |             |         |           |       |   |        |   |       |
|     |      |             |         |           |       |   |        |   |       |
|     |      |             |         |           |       |   |        |   |       |
|     |      |             |         |           |       |   |        |   |       |
|     |      |             |         |           |       |   |        |   |       |
|     |      |             |         |           |       |   |        |   |       |
|     |      |             |         |           |       |   |        |   |       |
|     |      |             |         |           |       |   |        |   |       |
|     |      |             |         |           |       |   |        |   |       |
|     |      |             |         |           |       |   |        |   |       |
|     |      |             |         |           |       |   |        |   |       |
|     |      |             |         |           |       |   |        |   |       |
|     |      |             |         |           |       |   |        |   |       |
|     |      |             |         |           |       |   |        |   |       |
|     |      |             |         |           |       |   |        |   |       |
|     |      |             |         |           |       |   |        |   |       |
|     |      |             |         |           |       |   |        |   |       |
|     |      |             |         |           |       |   |        |   |       |

# ACCOUNTING LEDGER

PAGE.No.

**Account Name And Number :**

**Year :** _____                                              **Month :** _____

| No. | Date | Description | Account | Reference | Debit | − | Credit | + | Total |
|-----|------|-------------|---------|-----------|-------|---|--------|---|-------|
| | | | | | | | | | |
| | | | | | | | | | |
| | | | | | | | | | |
| | | | | | | | | | |
| | | | | | | | | | |
| | | | | | | | | | |
| | | | | | | | | | |
| | | | | | | | | | |
| | | | | | | | | | |
| | | | | | | | | | |
| | | | | | | | | | |
| | | | | | | | | | |
| | | | | | | | | | |
| | | | | | | | | | |
| | | | | | | | | | |
| | | | | | | | | | |
| | | | | | | | | | |
| | | | | | | | | | |
| | | | | | | | | | |
| | | | | | | | | | |
| | | | | | | | | | |
| | | | | | | | | | |
| | | | | | | | | | |
| | | | | | | | | | |
| | | | | | | | | | |
| | | | | | | | | | |
| | | | | | | | | | |
| | | | | | | | | | |
| | | | | | | | | | |
| | | | | | | | | | |
| | | | | | | | | | |

# ACCOUNTING LEDGER

PAGE.No.

Account Name And Number :

Year : _____                                           Month : _____

| No. | Date | Description | Account | Reference | Debit | − | Credit | + | Total |
|-----|------|-------------|---------|-----------|-------|---|--------|---|-------|
| | | | | | | | | | |
| | | | | | | | | | |
| | | | | | | | | | |
| | | | | | | | | | |
| | | | | | | | | | |
| | | | | | | | | | |
| | | | | | | | | | |
| | | | | | | | | | |
| | | | | | | | | | |
| | | | | | | | | | |
| | | | | | | | | | |
| | | | | | | | | | |
| | | | | | | | | | |
| | | | | | | | | | |
| | | | | | | | | | |
| | | | | | | | | | |
| | | | | | | | | | |
| | | | | | | | | | |
| | | | | | | | | | |
| | | | | | | | | | |
| | | | | | | | | | |
| | | | | | | | | | |
| | | | | | | | | | |
| | | | | | | | | | |
| | | | | | | | | | |

# ACCOUNTING LEDGER

**PAGE.No.**

**Account Name And Number :**

**Year :** ____                                      **Month :** ____

| No. | Date | Description | Account | Reference | Debit | − | Credit | + | Total |
|-----|------|-------------|---------|-----------|-------|---|--------|---|-------|
|     |      |             |         |           |       |   |        |   |       |
|     |      |             |         |           |       |   |        |   |       |
|     |      |             |         |           |       |   |        |   |       |
|     |      |             |         |           |       |   |        |   |       |
|     |      |             |         |           |       |   |        |   |       |
|     |      |             |         |           |       |   |        |   |       |
|     |      |             |         |           |       |   |        |   |       |
|     |      |             |         |           |       |   |        |   |       |
|     |      |             |         |           |       |   |        |   |       |
|     |      |             |         |           |       |   |        |   |       |
|     |      |             |         |           |       |   |        |   |       |
|     |      |             |         |           |       |   |        |   |       |
|     |      |             |         |           |       |   |        |   |       |
|     |      |             |         |           |       |   |        |   |       |
|     |      |             |         |           |       |   |        |   |       |
|     |      |             |         |           |       |   |        |   |       |
|     |      |             |         |           |       |   |        |   |       |
|     |      |             |         |           |       |   |        |   |       |
|     |      |             |         |           |       |   |        |   |       |
|     |      |             |         |           |       |   |        |   |       |
|     |      |             |         |           |       |   |        |   |       |
|     |      |             |         |           |       |   |        |   |       |
|     |      |             |         |           |       |   |        |   |       |
|     |      |             |         |           |       |   |        |   |       |
|     |      |             |         |           |       |   |        |   |       |
|     |      |             |         |           |       |   |        |   |       |
|     |      |             |         |           |       |   |        |   |       |
|     |      |             |         |           |       |   |        |   |       |

# ACCOUNTING LEDGER

**PAGE.No.**

**Account Name And Number :**

**Year :** ____

**Month :** ____

| No. | Date | Description | Account | Reference | Debit | − | Credit | + | Total |
|-----|------|-------------|---------|-----------|-------|---|--------|---|-------|
|     |      |             |         |           |       |   |        |   |       |
|     |      |             |         |           |       |   |        |   |       |
|     |      |             |         |           |       |   |        |   |       |
|     |      |             |         |           |       |   |        |   |       |
|     |      |             |         |           |       |   |        |   |       |
|     |      |             |         |           |       |   |        |   |       |
|     |      |             |         |           |       |   |        |   |       |
|     |      |             |         |           |       |   |        |   |       |
|     |      |             |         |           |       |   |        |   |       |
|     |      |             |         |           |       |   |        |   |       |
|     |      |             |         |           |       |   |        |   |       |
|     |      |             |         |           |       |   |        |   |       |
|     |      |             |         |           |       |   |        |   |       |
|     |      |             |         |           |       |   |        |   |       |
|     |      |             |         |           |       |   |        |   |       |
|     |      |             |         |           |       |   |        |   |       |
|     |      |             |         |           |       |   |        |   |       |
|     |      |             |         |           |       |   |        |   |       |
|     |      |             |         |           |       |   |        |   |       |
|     |      |             |         |           |       |   |        |   |       |
|     |      |             |         |           |       |   |        |   |       |
|     |      |             |         |           |       |   |        |   |       |
|     |      |             |         |           |       |   |        |   |       |
|     |      |             |         |           |       |   |        |   |       |
|     |      |             |         |           |       |   |        |   |       |
|     |      |             |         |           |       |   |        |   |       |
|     |      |             |         |           |       |   |        |   |       |

# ACCOUNTING LEDGER

**PAGE.No.**

**Account Name And Number :**

**Year : _____**                              **Month : _____**

| No. | Date | Description | Account | Reference | Debit | − | Credit | + | Total |
|-----|------|-------------|---------|-----------|-------|---|--------|---|-------|
|     |      |             |         |           |       |   |        |   |       |
|     |      |             |         |           |       |   |        |   |       |
|     |      |             |         |           |       |   |        |   |       |
|     |      |             |         |           |       |   |        |   |       |
|     |      |             |         |           |       |   |        |   |       |
|     |      |             |         |           |       |   |        |   |       |
|     |      |             |         |           |       |   |        |   |       |
|     |      |             |         |           |       |   |        |   |       |
|     |      |             |         |           |       |   |        |   |       |
|     |      |             |         |           |       |   |        |   |       |
|     |      |             |         |           |       |   |        |   |       |
|     |      |             |         |           |       |   |        |   |       |
|     |      |             |         |           |       |   |        |   |       |
|     |      |             |         |           |       |   |        |   |       |
|     |      |             |         |           |       |   |        |   |       |
|     |      |             |         |           |       |   |        |   |       |
|     |      |             |         |           |       |   |        |   |       |
|     |      |             |         |           |       |   |        |   |       |
|     |      |             |         |           |       |   |        |   |       |
|     |      |             |         |           |       |   |        |   |       |
|     |      |             |         |           |       |   |        |   |       |
|     |      |             |         |           |       |   |        |   |       |
|     |      |             |         |           |       |   |        |   |       |
|     |      |             |         |           |       |   |        |   |       |
|     |      |             |         |           |       |   |        |   |       |
|     |      |             |         |           |       |   |        |   |       |
|     |      |             |         |           |       |   |        |   |       |
|     |      |             |         |           |       |   |        |   |       |
|     |      |             |         |           |       |   |        |   |       |
|     |      |             |         |           |       |   |        |   |       |

# ACCOUNTING LEDGER

**PAGE.No.**

**Account Name And Number :**

**Year : _____**                                          **Month : _____**

| No. | Date | Description | Account | Reference | Debit | − | Credit | + | Total |
|-----|------|-------------|---------|-----------|-------|---|--------|---|-------|
|     |      |             |         |           |       |   |        |   |       |
|     |      |             |         |           |       |   |        |   |       |
|     |      |             |         |           |       |   |        |   |       |
|     |      |             |         |           |       |   |        |   |       |
|     |      |             |         |           |       |   |        |   |       |
|     |      |             |         |           |       |   |        |   |       |
|     |      |             |         |           |       |   |        |   |       |
|     |      |             |         |           |       |   |        |   |       |
|     |      |             |         |           |       |   |        |   |       |
|     |      |             |         |           |       |   |        |   |       |
|     |      |             |         |           |       |   |        |   |       |
|     |      |             |         |           |       |   |        |   |       |
|     |      |             |         |           |       |   |        |   |       |
|     |      |             |         |           |       |   |        |   |       |
|     |      |             |         |           |       |   |        |   |       |
|     |      |             |         |           |       |   |        |   |       |
|     |      |             |         |           |       |   |        |   |       |
|     |      |             |         |           |       |   |        |   |       |
|     |      |             |         |           |       |   |        |   |       |
|     |      |             |         |           |       |   |        |   |       |
|     |      |             |         |           |       |   |        |   |       |
|     |      |             |         |           |       |   |        |   |       |
|     |      |             |         |           |       |   |        |   |       |
|     |      |             |         |           |       |   |        |   |       |
|     |      |             |         |           |       |   |        |   |       |
|     |      |             |         |           |       |   |        |   |       |
|     |      |             |         |           |       |   |        |   |       |

# ACCOUNTING LEDGER

**PAGE.No.**

**Account Name And Number :**

**Year : _____**                    **Month : _____**

| No. | Date | Description | Account | Reference | Debit | — | Credit | + | Total |
|-----|------|-------------|---------|-----------|-------|---|--------|---|-------|
|     |      |             |         |           |       |   |        |   |       |
|     |      |             |         |           |       |   |        |   |       |
|     |      |             |         |           |       |   |        |   |       |
|     |      |             |         |           |       |   |        |   |       |
|     |      |             |         |           |       |   |        |   |       |
|     |      |             |         |           |       |   |        |   |       |
|     |      |             |         |           |       |   |        |   |       |
|     |      |             |         |           |       |   |        |   |       |
|     |      |             |         |           |       |   |        |   |       |
|     |      |             |         |           |       |   |        |   |       |
|     |      |             |         |           |       |   |        |   |       |
|     |      |             |         |           |       |   |        |   |       |
|     |      |             |         |           |       |   |        |   |       |
|     |      |             |         |           |       |   |        |   |       |
|     |      |             |         |           |       |   |        |   |       |
|     |      |             |         |           |       |   |        |   |       |
|     |      |             |         |           |       |   |        |   |       |
|     |      |             |         |           |       |   |        |   |       |
|     |      |             |         |           |       |   |        |   |       |
|     |      |             |         |           |       |   |        |   |       |
|     |      |             |         |           |       |   |        |   |       |
|     |      |             |         |           |       |   |        |   |       |
|     |      |             |         |           |       |   |        |   |       |
|     |      |             |         |           |       |   |        |   |       |
|     |      |             |         |           |       |   |        |   |       |
|     |      |             |         |           |       |   |        |   |       |
|     |      |             |         |           |       |   |        |   |       |
|     |      |             |         |           |       |   |        |   |       |
|     |      |             |         |           |       |   |        |   |       |

# ACCOUNTING LEDGER

**PAGE.No.**

**Account Name And Number :**

**Year : _____**　　　　　　　　　　　**Month : _____**

| No. | Date | Description | Account | Reference | Debit | − | Credit | + | Total |
|-----|------|-------------|---------|-----------|-------|---|--------|---|-------|
|  |  |  |  |  |  |  |  |  |  |
|  |  |  |  |  |  |  |  |  |  |
|  |  |  |  |  |  |  |  |  |  |
|  |  |  |  |  |  |  |  |  |  |
|  |  |  |  |  |  |  |  |  |  |
|  |  |  |  |  |  |  |  |  |  |
|  |  |  |  |  |  |  |  |  |  |
|  |  |  |  |  |  |  |  |  |  |
|  |  |  |  |  |  |  |  |  |  |
|  |  |  |  |  |  |  |  |  |  |
|  |  |  |  |  |  |  |  |  |  |
|  |  |  |  |  |  |  |  |  |  |
|  |  |  |  |  |  |  |  |  |  |
|  |  |  |  |  |  |  |  |  |  |
|  |  |  |  |  |  |  |  |  |  |
|  |  |  |  |  |  |  |  |  |  |
|  |  |  |  |  |  |  |  |  |  |
|  |  |  |  |  |  |  |  |  |  |
|  |  |  |  |  |  |  |  |  |  |
|  |  |  |  |  |  |  |  |  |  |
|  |  |  |  |  |  |  |  |  |  |
|  |  |  |  |  |  |  |  |  |  |
|  |  |  |  |  |  |  |  |  |  |
|  |  |  |  |  |  |  |  |  |  |
|  |  |  |  |  |  |  |  |  |  |
|  |  |  |  |  |  |  |  |  |  |
|  |  |  |  |  |  |  |  |  |  |
|  |  |  |  |  |  |  |  |  |  |
|  |  |  |  |  |  |  |  |  |  |
|  |  |  |  |  |  |  |  |  |  |

# ACCOUNTING LEDGER

PAGE.No.

**Account Name And Number :**

Year : _____                                    Month : _____

| No. | Date | Description | Account | Reference | Debit | − | Credit | + | Total |
|-----|------|-------------|---------|-----------|-------|---|--------|---|-------|
|     |      |             |         |           |       |   |        |   |       |
|     |      |             |         |           |       |   |        |   |       |
|     |      |             |         |           |       |   |        |   |       |
|     |      |             |         |           |       |   |        |   |       |
|     |      |             |         |           |       |   |        |   |       |
|     |      |             |         |           |       |   |        |   |       |
|     |      |             |         |           |       |   |        |   |       |
|     |      |             |         |           |       |   |        |   |       |
|     |      |             |         |           |       |   |        |   |       |
|     |      |             |         |           |       |   |        |   |       |
|     |      |             |         |           |       |   |        |   |       |
|     |      |             |         |           |       |   |        |   |       |
|     |      |             |         |           |       |   |        |   |       |
|     |      |             |         |           |       |   |        |   |       |
|     |      |             |         |           |       |   |        |   |       |
|     |      |             |         |           |       |   |        |   |       |
|     |      |             |         |           |       |   |        |   |       |
|     |      |             |         |           |       |   |        |   |       |
|     |      |             |         |           |       |   |        |   |       |
|     |      |             |         |           |       |   |        |   |       |
|     |      |             |         |           |       |   |        |   |       |
|     |      |             |         |           |       |   |        |   |       |
|     |      |             |         |           |       |   |        |   |       |
|     |      |             |         |           |       |   |        |   |       |
|     |      |             |         |           |       |   |        |   |       |
|     |      |             |         |           |       |   |        |   |       |
|     |      |             |         |           |       |   |        |   |       |

# ACCOUNTING LEDGER

PAGE.No.

**Account Name And Number :**

**Year :** _____          **Month :** _____

| No. | Date | Description | Account | Reference | Debit | − | Credit | + | Total |
|-----|------|-------------|---------|-----------|-------|---|--------|---|-------|
|  |  |  |  |  |  |  |  |  |  |
|  |  |  |  |  |  |  |  |  |  |
|  |  |  |  |  |  |  |  |  |  |
|  |  |  |  |  |  |  |  |  |  |
|  |  |  |  |  |  |  |  |  |  |
|  |  |  |  |  |  |  |  |  |  |
|  |  |  |  |  |  |  |  |  |  |
|  |  |  |  |  |  |  |  |  |  |
|  |  |  |  |  |  |  |  |  |  |
|  |  |  |  |  |  |  |  |  |  |
|  |  |  |  |  |  |  |  |  |  |
|  |  |  |  |  |  |  |  |  |  |
|  |  |  |  |  |  |  |  |  |  |
|  |  |  |  |  |  |  |  |  |  |
|  |  |  |  |  |  |  |  |  |  |
|  |  |  |  |  |  |  |  |  |  |
|  |  |  |  |  |  |  |  |  |  |
|  |  |  |  |  |  |  |  |  |  |
|  |  |  |  |  |  |  |  |  |  |
|  |  |  |  |  |  |  |  |  |  |
|  |  |  |  |  |  |  |  |  |  |
|  |  |  |  |  |  |  |  |  |  |
|  |  |  |  |  |  |  |  |  |  |
|  |  |  |  |  |  |  |  |  |  |
|  |  |  |  |  |  |  |  |  |  |
|  |  |  |  |  |  |  |  |  |  |
|  |  |  |  |  |  |  |  |  |  |
|  |  |  |  |  |  |  |  |  |  |
|  |  |  |  |  |  |  |  |  |  |

# ACCOUNTING LEDGER

**PAGE.No.**

**Account Name And Number :**

**Year :** _____                                          **Month :** _____

| No. | Date | Description | Account | Reference | Debit | − | Credit | + | Total |
|-----|------|-------------|---------|-----------|-------|---|--------|---|-------|
|     |      |             |         |           |       |   |        |   |       |
|     |      |             |         |           |       |   |        |   |       |
|     |      |             |         |           |       |   |        |   |       |
|     |      |             |         |           |       |   |        |   |       |
|     |      |             |         |           |       |   |        |   |       |
|     |      |             |         |           |       |   |        |   |       |
|     |      |             |         |           |       |   |        |   |       |
|     |      |             |         |           |       |   |        |   |       |
|     |      |             |         |           |       |   |        |   |       |
|     |      |             |         |           |       |   |        |   |       |
|     |      |             |         |           |       |   |        |   |       |
|     |      |             |         |           |       |   |        |   |       |
|     |      |             |         |           |       |   |        |   |       |
|     |      |             |         |           |       |   |        |   |       |
|     |      |             |         |           |       |   |        |   |       |
|     |      |             |         |           |       |   |        |   |       |
|     |      |             |         |           |       |   |        |   |       |
|     |      |             |         |           |       |   |        |   |       |
|     |      |             |         |           |       |   |        |   |       |
|     |      |             |         |           |       |   |        |   |       |
|     |      |             |         |           |       |   |        |   |       |
|     |      |             |         |           |       |   |        |   |       |
|     |      |             |         |           |       |   |        |   |       |
|     |      |             |         |           |       |   |        |   |       |
|     |      |             |         |           |       |   |        |   |       |
|     |      |             |         |           |       |   |        |   |       |
|     |      |             |         |           |       |   |        |   |       |

# ACCOUNTING LEDGER

PAGE.No.

**Account Name And Number :**

**Year : _____**                                    **Month : _____**

| No. | Date | Description | Account | Reference | Debit | − | Credit | + | Total |
|-----|------|-------------|---------|-----------|-------|---|--------|---|-------|
|     |      |             |         |           |       |   |        |   |       |
|     |      |             |         |           |       |   |        |   |       |
|     |      |             |         |           |       |   |        |   |       |
|     |      |             |         |           |       |   |        |   |       |
|     |      |             |         |           |       |   |        |   |       |
|     |      |             |         |           |       |   |        |   |       |
|     |      |             |         |           |       |   |        |   |       |
|     |      |             |         |           |       |   |        |   |       |
|     |      |             |         |           |       |   |        |   |       |
|     |      |             |         |           |       |   |        |   |       |
|     |      |             |         |           |       |   |        |   |       |
|     |      |             |         |           |       |   |        |   |       |
|     |      |             |         |           |       |   |        |   |       |
|     |      |             |         |           |       |   |        |   |       |
|     |      |             |         |           |       |   |        |   |       |
|     |      |             |         |           |       |   |        |   |       |
|     |      |             |         |           |       |   |        |   |       |
|     |      |             |         |           |       |   |        |   |       |
|     |      |             |         |           |       |   |        |   |       |
|     |      |             |         |           |       |   |        |   |       |
|     |      |             |         |           |       |   |        |   |       |
|     |      |             |         |           |       |   |        |   |       |
|     |      |             |         |           |       |   |        |   |       |
|     |      |             |         |           |       |   |        |   |       |
|     |      |             |         |           |       |   |        |   |       |
|     |      |             |         |           |       |   |        |   |       |

# ACCOUNTING LEDGER

**PAGE.No.**

**Account Name And Number :**

**Year : _____**                                    **Month : _____**

| No. | Date | Description | Account | Reference | Debit | − | Credit | + | Total |
|-----|------|-------------|---------|-----------|-------|---|--------|---|-------|
|     |      |             |         |           |       |   |        |   |       |
|     |      |             |         |           |       |   |        |   |       |
|     |      |             |         |           |       |   |        |   |       |
|     |      |             |         |           |       |   |        |   |       |
|     |      |             |         |           |       |   |        |   |       |
|     |      |             |         |           |       |   |        |   |       |
|     |      |             |         |           |       |   |        |   |       |
|     |      |             |         |           |       |   |        |   |       |
|     |      |             |         |           |       |   |        |   |       |
|     |      |             |         |           |       |   |        |   |       |
|     |      |             |         |           |       |   |        |   |       |
|     |      |             |         |           |       |   |        |   |       |
|     |      |             |         |           |       |   |        |   |       |
|     |      |             |         |           |       |   |        |   |       |
|     |      |             |         |           |       |   |        |   |       |
|     |      |             |         |           |       |   |        |   |       |
|     |      |             |         |           |       |   |        |   |       |
|     |      |             |         |           |       |   |        |   |       |
|     |      |             |         |           |       |   |        |   |       |
|     |      |             |         |           |       |   |        |   |       |
|     |      |             |         |           |       |   |        |   |       |
|     |      |             |         |           |       |   |        |   |       |
|     |      |             |         |           |       |   |        |   |       |
|     |      |             |         |           |       |   |        |   |       |
|     |      |             |         |           |       |   |        |   |       |
|     |      |             |         |           |       |   |        |   |       |
|     |      |             |         |           |       |   |        |   |       |

# ACCOUNTING LEDGER

PAGE.No.

Account Name And Number :

Year : ____                                    Month : ____

| No. | Date | Description | Account | Reference | Debit | − | Credit | + | Total |
|-----|------|-------------|---------|-----------|-------|---|--------|---|-------|
|     |      |             |         |           |       |   |        |   |       |
|     |      |             |         |           |       |   |        |   |       |
|     |      |             |         |           |       |   |        |   |       |
|     |      |             |         |           |       |   |        |   |       |
|     |      |             |         |           |       |   |        |   |       |
|     |      |             |         |           |       |   |        |   |       |
|     |      |             |         |           |       |   |        |   |       |
|     |      |             |         |           |       |   |        |   |       |
|     |      |             |         |           |       |   |        |   |       |
|     |      |             |         |           |       |   |        |   |       |
|     |      |             |         |           |       |   |        |   |       |
|     |      |             |         |           |       |   |        |   |       |
|     |      |             |         |           |       |   |        |   |       |
|     |      |             |         |           |       |   |        |   |       |
|     |      |             |         |           |       |   |        |   |       |
|     |      |             |         |           |       |   |        |   |       |
|     |      |             |         |           |       |   |        |   |       |
|     |      |             |         |           |       |   |        |   |       |
|     |      |             |         |           |       |   |        |   |       |
|     |      |             |         |           |       |   |        |   |       |
|     |      |             |         |           |       |   |        |   |       |
|     |      |             |         |           |       |   |        |   |       |
|     |      |             |         |           |       |   |        |   |       |
|     |      |             |         |           |       |   |        |   |       |
|     |      |             |         |           |       |   |        |   |       |
|     |      |             |         |           |       |   |        |   |       |
|     |      |             |         |           |       |   |        |   |       |

# ACCOUNTING LEDGER

PAGE.No.

Account Name And Number :

Year : _____                                           Month : _____

| No. | Date | Description | Account | Reference | Debit | — | Credit | + | Total |
|-----|------|-------------|---------|-----------|-------|---|--------|---|-------|
|     |      |             |         |           |       |   |        |   |       |
|     |      |             |         |           |       |   |        |   |       |
|     |      |             |         |           |       |   |        |   |       |
|     |      |             |         |           |       |   |        |   |       |
|     |      |             |         |           |       |   |        |   |       |
|     |      |             |         |           |       |   |        |   |       |
|     |      |             |         |           |       |   |        |   |       |
|     |      |             |         |           |       |   |        |   |       |
|     |      |             |         |           |       |   |        |   |       |
|     |      |             |         |           |       |   |        |   |       |
|     |      |             |         |           |       |   |        |   |       |
|     |      |             |         |           |       |   |        |   |       |
|     |      |             |         |           |       |   |        |   |       |
|     |      |             |         |           |       |   |        |   |       |
|     |      |             |         |           |       |   |        |   |       |
|     |      |             |         |           |       |   |        |   |       |
|     |      |             |         |           |       |   |        |   |       |
|     |      |             |         |           |       |   |        |   |       |
|     |      |             |         |           |       |   |        |   |       |
|     |      |             |         |           |       |   |        |   |       |
|     |      |             |         |           |       |   |        |   |       |
|     |      |             |         |           |       |   |        |   |       |
|     |      |             |         |           |       |   |        |   |       |
|     |      |             |         |           |       |   |        |   |       |
|     |      |             |         |           |       |   |        |   |       |
|     |      |             |         |           |       |   |        |   |       |
|     |      |             |         |           |       |   |        |   |       |
|     |      |             |         |           |       |   |        |   |       |

# ACCOUNTING LEDGER

**PAGE.No.**

**Account Name And Number :**

**Year : _____**                                          **Month : _____**

| No. | Date | Description | Account | Reference | Debit | − | Credit | + | Total |
|-----|------|-------------|---------|-----------|-------|---|--------|---|-------|
|     |      |             |         |           |       |   |        |   |       |
|     |      |             |         |           |       |   |        |   |       |
|     |      |             |         |           |       |   |        |   |       |
|     |      |             |         |           |       |   |        |   |       |
|     |      |             |         |           |       |   |        |   |       |
|     |      |             |         |           |       |   |        |   |       |
|     |      |             |         |           |       |   |        |   |       |
|     |      |             |         |           |       |   |        |   |       |
|     |      |             |         |           |       |   |        |   |       |
|     |      |             |         |           |       |   |        |   |       |
|     |      |             |         |           |       |   |        |   |       |
|     |      |             |         |           |       |   |        |   |       |
|     |      |             |         |           |       |   |        |   |       |
|     |      |             |         |           |       |   |        |   |       |
|     |      |             |         |           |       |   |        |   |       |
|     |      |             |         |           |       |   |        |   |       |
|     |      |             |         |           |       |   |        |   |       |
|     |      |             |         |           |       |   |        |   |       |
|     |      |             |         |           |       |   |        |   |       |
|     |      |             |         |           |       |   |        |   |       |
|     |      |             |         |           |       |   |        |   |       |
|     |      |             |         |           |       |   |        |   |       |
|     |      |             |         |           |       |   |        |   |       |
|     |      |             |         |           |       |   |        |   |       |
|     |      |             |         |           |       |   |        |   |       |
|     |      |             |         |           |       |   |        |   |       |

# ACCOUNTING LEDGER

PAGE.No.

**Account Name And Number :**

**Year : _____**                              **Month : _____**

| No. | Date | Description | Account | Reference | Debit | − | Credit | + | Total |
|-----|------|-------------|---------|-----------|-------|---|--------|---|-------|
|     |      |             |         |           |       |   |        |   |       |
|     |      |             |         |           |       |   |        |   |       |
|     |      |             |         |           |       |   |        |   |       |
|     |      |             |         |           |       |   |        |   |       |
|     |      |             |         |           |       |   |        |   |       |
|     |      |             |         |           |       |   |        |   |       |
|     |      |             |         |           |       |   |        |   |       |
|     |      |             |         |           |       |   |        |   |       |
|     |      |             |         |           |       |   |        |   |       |
|     |      |             |         |           |       |   |        |   |       |
|     |      |             |         |           |       |   |        |   |       |
|     |      |             |         |           |       |   |        |   |       |
|     |      |             |         |           |       |   |        |   |       |
|     |      |             |         |           |       |   |        |   |       |
|     |      |             |         |           |       |   |        |   |       |
|     |      |             |         |           |       |   |        |   |       |
|     |      |             |         |           |       |   |        |   |       |
|     |      |             |         |           |       |   |        |   |       |
|     |      |             |         |           |       |   |        |   |       |
|     |      |             |         |           |       |   |        |   |       |
|     |      |             |         |           |       |   |        |   |       |
|     |      |             |         |           |       |   |        |   |       |
|     |      |             |         |           |       |   |        |   |       |
|     |      |             |         |           |       |   |        |   |       |
|     |      |             |         |           |       |   |        |   |       |
|     |      |             |         |           |       |   |        |   |       |
|     |      |             |         |           |       |   |        |   |       |
|     |      |             |         |           |       |   |        |   |       |

# ACCOUNTING LEDGER

PAGE.No.

Account Name And Number :

Year : _____                                                    Month : _____

| No. | Date | Description | Account | Reference | Debit | − | Credit | + | Total |
|-----|------|-------------|---------|-----------|-------|---|--------|---|-------|
|     |      |             |         |           |       |   |        |   |       |
|     |      |             |         |           |       |   |        |   |       |
|     |      |             |         |           |       |   |        |   |       |
|     |      |             |         |           |       |   |        |   |       |
|     |      |             |         |           |       |   |        |   |       |
|     |      |             |         |           |       |   |        |   |       |
|     |      |             |         |           |       |   |        |   |       |
|     |      |             |         |           |       |   |        |   |       |
|     |      |             |         |           |       |   |        |   |       |
|     |      |             |         |           |       |   |        |   |       |
|     |      |             |         |           |       |   |        |   |       |
|     |      |             |         |           |       |   |        |   |       |
|     |      |             |         |           |       |   |        |   |       |
|     |      |             |         |           |       |   |        |   |       |
|     |      |             |         |           |       |   |        |   |       |
|     |      |             |         |           |       |   |        |   |       |
|     |      |             |         |           |       |   |        |   |       |
|     |      |             |         |           |       |   |        |   |       |
|     |      |             |         |           |       |   |        |   |       |
|     |      |             |         |           |       |   |        |   |       |
|     |      |             |         |           |       |   |        |   |       |
|     |      |             |         |           |       |   |        |   |       |
|     |      |             |         |           |       |   |        |   |       |
|     |      |             |         |           |       |   |        |   |       |
|     |      |             |         |           |       |   |        |   |       |
|     |      |             |         |           |       |   |        |   |       |

# ACCOUNTING LEDGER

**PAGE.No.**

**Account Name And Number :**

**Year :** _____          **Month :** _____

| No. | Date | Description | Account | Reference | Debit | − | Credit | + | Total |
|-----|------|-------------|---------|-----------|-------|---|--------|---|-------|
|     |      |             |         |           |       |   |        |   |       |
|     |      |             |         |           |       |   |        |   |       |
|     |      |             |         |           |       |   |        |   |       |
|     |      |             |         |           |       |   |        |   |       |
|     |      |             |         |           |       |   |        |   |       |
|     |      |             |         |           |       |   |        |   |       |
|     |      |             |         |           |       |   |        |   |       |
|     |      |             |         |           |       |   |        |   |       |
|     |      |             |         |           |       |   |        |   |       |
|     |      |             |         |           |       |   |        |   |       |
|     |      |             |         |           |       |   |        |   |       |
|     |      |             |         |           |       |   |        |   |       |
|     |      |             |         |           |       |   |        |   |       |
|     |      |             |         |           |       |   |        |   |       |
|     |      |             |         |           |       |   |        |   |       |
|     |      |             |         |           |       |   |        |   |       |
|     |      |             |         |           |       |   |        |   |       |
|     |      |             |         |           |       |   |        |   |       |
|     |      |             |         |           |       |   |        |   |       |
|     |      |             |         |           |       |   |        |   |       |
|     |      |             |         |           |       |   |        |   |       |
|     |      |             |         |           |       |   |        |   |       |
|     |      |             |         |           |       |   |        |   |       |
|     |      |             |         |           |       |   |        |   |       |
|     |      |             |         |           |       |   |        |   |       |

# ACCOUNTING LEDGER

**PAGE.No.**

**Account Name And Number :**

**Year : _____**                                      **Month : _____**

| No. | Date | Description | Account | Reference | Debit | − | Credit | + | Total |
|-----|------|-------------|---------|-----------|-------|---|--------|---|-------|
|     |      |             |         |           |       |   |        |   |       |
|     |      |             |         |           |       |   |        |   |       |
|     |      |             |         |           |       |   |        |   |       |
|     |      |             |         |           |       |   |        |   |       |
|     |      |             |         |           |       |   |        |   |       |
|     |      |             |         |           |       |   |        |   |       |
|     |      |             |         |           |       |   |        |   |       |
|     |      |             |         |           |       |   |        |   |       |
|     |      |             |         |           |       |   |        |   |       |
|     |      |             |         |           |       |   |        |   |       |
|     |      |             |         |           |       |   |        |   |       |
|     |      |             |         |           |       |   |        |   |       |
|     |      |             |         |           |       |   |        |   |       |
|     |      |             |         |           |       |   |        |   |       |
|     |      |             |         |           |       |   |        |   |       |
|     |      |             |         |           |       |   |        |   |       |
|     |      |             |         |           |       |   |        |   |       |
|     |      |             |         |           |       |   |        |   |       |
|     |      |             |         |           |       |   |        |   |       |
|     |      |             |         |           |       |   |        |   |       |
|     |      |             |         |           |       |   |        |   |       |
|     |      |             |         |           |       |   |        |   |       |
|     |      |             |         |           |       |   |        |   |       |
|     |      |             |         |           |       |   |        |   |       |
|     |      |             |         |           |       |   |        |   |       |
|     |      |             |         |           |       |   |        |   |       |
|     |      |             |         |           |       |   |        |   |       |
|     |      |             |         |           |       |   |        |   |       |

# ACCOUNTING LEDGER

**PAGE.No.**

**Account Name And Number :**

**Year :** _____     **Month :** _____

| No. | Date | Description | Account | Reference | Debit | — | Credit | + | Total |
|-----|------|-------------|---------|-----------|-------|---|--------|---|-------|
|     |      |             |         |           |       |   |        |   |       |
|     |      |             |         |           |       |   |        |   |       |
|     |      |             |         |           |       |   |        |   |       |
|     |      |             |         |           |       |   |        |   |       |
|     |      |             |         |           |       |   |        |   |       |
|     |      |             |         |           |       |   |        |   |       |
|     |      |             |         |           |       |   |        |   |       |
|     |      |             |         |           |       |   |        |   |       |
|     |      |             |         |           |       |   |        |   |       |
|     |      |             |         |           |       |   |        |   |       |
|     |      |             |         |           |       |   |        |   |       |
|     |      |             |         |           |       |   |        |   |       |
|     |      |             |         |           |       |   |        |   |       |
|     |      |             |         |           |       |   |        |   |       |
|     |      |             |         |           |       |   |        |   |       |
|     |      |             |         |           |       |   |        |   |       |
|     |      |             |         |           |       |   |        |   |       |
|     |      |             |         |           |       |   |        |   |       |
|     |      |             |         |           |       |   |        |   |       |
|     |      |             |         |           |       |   |        |   |       |
|     |      |             |         |           |       |   |        |   |       |
|     |      |             |         |           |       |   |        |   |       |
|     |      |             |         |           |       |   |        |   |       |
|     |      |             |         |           |       |   |        |   |       |
|     |      |             |         |           |       |   |        |   |       |
|     |      |             |         |           |       |   |        |   |       |
|     |      |             |         |           |       |   |        |   |       |
|     |      |             |         |           |       |   |        |   |       |

# ACCOUNTING LEDGER

PAGE.No.

Account Name And Number :

Year : _____                                    Month : _____

| No. | Date | Description | Account | Reference | Debit | − | Credit | + | Total |
|-----|------|-------------|---------|-----------|-------|---|--------|---|-------|
|     |      |             |         |           |       |   |        |   |       |
|     |      |             |         |           |       |   |        |   |       |
|     |      |             |         |           |       |   |        |   |       |
|     |      |             |         |           |       |   |        |   |       |
|     |      |             |         |           |       |   |        |   |       |
|     |      |             |         |           |       |   |        |   |       |
|     |      |             |         |           |       |   |        |   |       |
|     |      |             |         |           |       |   |        |   |       |
|     |      |             |         |           |       |   |        |   |       |
|     |      |             |         |           |       |   |        |   |       |
|     |      |             |         |           |       |   |        |   |       |
|     |      |             |         |           |       |   |        |   |       |
|     |      |             |         |           |       |   |        |   |       |
|     |      |             |         |           |       |   |        |   |       |
|     |      |             |         |           |       |   |        |   |       |
|     |      |             |         |           |       |   |        |   |       |
|     |      |             |         |           |       |   |        |   |       |
|     |      |             |         |           |       |   |        |   |       |
|     |      |             |         |           |       |   |        |   |       |
|     |      |             |         |           |       |   |        |   |       |
|     |      |             |         |           |       |   |        |   |       |
|     |      |             |         |           |       |   |        |   |       |
|     |      |             |         |           |       |   |        |   |       |
|     |      |             |         |           |       |   |        |   |       |
|     |      |             |         |           |       |   |        |   |       |
|     |      |             |         |           |       |   |        |   |       |
|     |      |             |         |           |       |   |        |   |       |
|     |      |             |         |           |       |   |        |   |       |
|     |      |             |         |           |       |   |        |   |       |

# ACCOUNTING LEDGER

PAGE.No.

Account Name And Number :

Year : _____                                Month : _____

| No. | Date | Description | Account | Reference | Debit | − | Credit | + | Total |
|-----|------|-------------|---------|-----------|-------|---|--------|---|-------|
|     |      |             |         |           |       |   |        |   |       |
|     |      |             |         |           |       |   |        |   |       |
|     |      |             |         |           |       |   |        |   |       |
|     |      |             |         |           |       |   |        |   |       |
|     |      |             |         |           |       |   |        |   |       |
|     |      |             |         |           |       |   |        |   |       |
|     |      |             |         |           |       |   |        |   |       |
|     |      |             |         |           |       |   |        |   |       |
|     |      |             |         |           |       |   |        |   |       |
|     |      |             |         |           |       |   |        |   |       |
|     |      |             |         |           |       |   |        |   |       |
|     |      |             |         |           |       |   |        |   |       |
|     |      |             |         |           |       |   |        |   |       |
|     |      |             |         |           |       |   |        |   |       |
|     |      |             |         |           |       |   |        |   |       |
|     |      |             |         |           |       |   |        |   |       |
|     |      |             |         |           |       |   |        |   |       |
|     |      |             |         |           |       |   |        |   |       |
|     |      |             |         |           |       |   |        |   |       |
|     |      |             |         |           |       |   |        |   |       |
|     |      |             |         |           |       |   |        |   |       |
|     |      |             |         |           |       |   |        |   |       |
|     |      |             |         |           |       |   |        |   |       |
|     |      |             |         |           |       |   |        |   |       |
|     |      |             |         |           |       |   |        |   |       |
|     |      |             |         |           |       |   |        |   |       |
|     |      |             |         |           |       |   |        |   |       |
|     |      |             |         |           |       |   |        |   |       |
|     |      |             |         |           |       |   |        |   |       |

# ACCOUNTING LEDGER

**PAGE.No.**

**Account Name And Number :**

**Year : _____**                    **Month : _____**

| No. | Date | Description | Account | Reference | Debit | − | Credit | + | Total |
|-----|------|-------------|---------|-----------|-------|---|--------|---|-------|
|     |      |             |         |           |       |   |        |   |       |
|     |      |             |         |           |       |   |        |   |       |
|     |      |             |         |           |       |   |        |   |       |
|     |      |             |         |           |       |   |        |   |       |
|     |      |             |         |           |       |   |        |   |       |
|     |      |             |         |           |       |   |        |   |       |
|     |      |             |         |           |       |   |        |   |       |
|     |      |             |         |           |       |   |        |   |       |
|     |      |             |         |           |       |   |        |   |       |
|     |      |             |         |           |       |   |        |   |       |
|     |      |             |         |           |       |   |        |   |       |
|     |      |             |         |           |       |   |        |   |       |
|     |      |             |         |           |       |   |        |   |       |
|     |      |             |         |           |       |   |        |   |       |
|     |      |             |         |           |       |   |        |   |       |
|     |      |             |         |           |       |   |        |   |       |
|     |      |             |         |           |       |   |        |   |       |
|     |      |             |         |           |       |   |        |   |       |
|     |      |             |         |           |       |   |        |   |       |
|     |      |             |         |           |       |   |        |   |       |
|     |      |             |         |           |       |   |        |   |       |
|     |      |             |         |           |       |   |        |   |       |
|     |      |             |         |           |       |   |        |   |       |
|     |      |             |         |           |       |   |        |   |       |
|     |      |             |         |           |       |   |        |   |       |
|     |      |             |         |           |       |   |        |   |       |
|     |      |             |         |           |       |   |        |   |       |

# ACCOUNTING LEDGER

**PAGE.No.** _____

**Account Name And Number :** _____

**Year :** _____          **Month :** _____

| No. | Date | Description | Account | Reference | Debit | − | Credit | + | Total |
|-----|------|-------------|---------|-----------|-------|---|--------|---|-------|
|     |      |             |         |           |       |   |        |   |       |
|     |      |             |         |           |       |   |        |   |       |
|     |      |             |         |           |       |   |        |   |       |
|     |      |             |         |           |       |   |        |   |       |
|     |      |             |         |           |       |   |        |   |       |
|     |      |             |         |           |       |   |        |   |       |
|     |      |             |         |           |       |   |        |   |       |
|     |      |             |         |           |       |   |        |   |       |
|     |      |             |         |           |       |   |        |   |       |
|     |      |             |         |           |       |   |        |   |       |
|     |      |             |         |           |       |   |        |   |       |
|     |      |             |         |           |       |   |        |   |       |
|     |      |             |         |           |       |   |        |   |       |
|     |      |             |         |           |       |   |        |   |       |
|     |      |             |         |           |       |   |        |   |       |
|     |      |             |         |           |       |   |        |   |       |
|     |      |             |         |           |       |   |        |   |       |
|     |      |             |         |           |       |   |        |   |       |
|     |      |             |         |           |       |   |        |   |       |
|     |      |             |         |           |       |   |        |   |       |
|     |      |             |         |           |       |   |        |   |       |
|     |      |             |         |           |       |   |        |   |       |
|     |      |             |         |           |       |   |        |   |       |
|     |      |             |         |           |       |   |        |   |       |
|     |      |             |         |           |       |   |        |   |       |
|     |      |             |         |           |       |   |        |   |       |
|     |      |             |         |           |       |   |        |   |       |
|     |      |             |         |           |       |   |        |   |       |

# ACCOUNTING LEDGER

PAGE.No.

**Account Name And Number :**

**Year : _____**                                         **Month : _____**

| No. | Date | Description | Account | Reference | Debit | − | Credit | + | Total |
|-----|------|-------------|---------|-----------|-------|---|--------|---|-------|
|     |      |             |         |           |       |   |        |   |       |
|     |      |             |         |           |       |   |        |   |       |
|     |      |             |         |           |       |   |        |   |       |
|     |      |             |         |           |       |   |        |   |       |
|     |      |             |         |           |       |   |        |   |       |
|     |      |             |         |           |       |   |        |   |       |
|     |      |             |         |           |       |   |        |   |       |
|     |      |             |         |           |       |   |        |   |       |
|     |      |             |         |           |       |   |        |   |       |
|     |      |             |         |           |       |   |        |   |       |
|     |      |             |         |           |       |   |        |   |       |
|     |      |             |         |           |       |   |        |   |       |
|     |      |             |         |           |       |   |        |   |       |
|     |      |             |         |           |       |   |        |   |       |
|     |      |             |         |           |       |   |        |   |       |
|     |      |             |         |           |       |   |        |   |       |
|     |      |             |         |           |       |   |        |   |       |
|     |      |             |         |           |       |   |        |   |       |
|     |      |             |         |           |       |   |        |   |       |
|     |      |             |         |           |       |   |        |   |       |
|     |      |             |         |           |       |   |        |   |       |
|     |      |             |         |           |       |   |        |   |       |
|     |      |             |         |           |       |   |        |   |       |
|     |      |             |         |           |       |   |        |   |       |
|     |      |             |         |           |       |   |        |   |       |
|     |      |             |         |           |       |   |        |   |       |
|     |      |             |         |           |       |   |        |   |       |
|     |      |             |         |           |       |   |        |   |       |

# ACCOUNTING LEDGER

PAGE.No.

Account Name And Number :

Year : _____                                          Month : _____

| No. | Date | Description | Account | Reference | Debit | − | Credit | + | Total |
|-----|------|-------------|---------|-----------|-------|---|--------|---|-------|
|     |      |             |         |           |       |   |        |   |       |
|     |      |             |         |           |       |   |        |   |       |
|     |      |             |         |           |       |   |        |   |       |
|     |      |             |         |           |       |   |        |   |       |
|     |      |             |         |           |       |   |        |   |       |
|     |      |             |         |           |       |   |        |   |       |
|     |      |             |         |           |       |   |        |   |       |
|     |      |             |         |           |       |   |        |   |       |
|     |      |             |         |           |       |   |        |   |       |
|     |      |             |         |           |       |   |        |   |       |
|     |      |             |         |           |       |   |        |   |       |
|     |      |             |         |           |       |   |        |   |       |
|     |      |             |         |           |       |   |        |   |       |
|     |      |             |         |           |       |   |        |   |       |
|     |      |             |         |           |       |   |        |   |       |
|     |      |             |         |           |       |   |        |   |       |
|     |      |             |         |           |       |   |        |   |       |
|     |      |             |         |           |       |   |        |   |       |
|     |      |             |         |           |       |   |        |   |       |
|     |      |             |         |           |       |   |        |   |       |
|     |      |             |         |           |       |   |        |   |       |
|     |      |             |         |           |       |   |        |   |       |
|     |      |             |         |           |       |   |        |   |       |
|     |      |             |         |           |       |   |        |   |       |
|     |      |             |         |           |       |   |        |   |       |
|     |      |             |         |           |       |   |        |   |       |

# ACCOUNTING LEDGER

**PAGE.No.**

**Account Name And Number :**

**Year : _____**                                              **Month : _____**

| No. | Date | Description | Account | Reference | Debit | − | Credit | + | Total |
|-----|------|-------------|---------|-----------|-------|---|--------|---|-------|
|     |      |             |         |           |       |   |        |   |       |
|     |      |             |         |           |       |   |        |   |       |
|     |      |             |         |           |       |   |        |   |       |
|     |      |             |         |           |       |   |        |   |       |
|     |      |             |         |           |       |   |        |   |       |
|     |      |             |         |           |       |   |        |   |       |
|     |      |             |         |           |       |   |        |   |       |
|     |      |             |         |           |       |   |        |   |       |
|     |      |             |         |           |       |   |        |   |       |
|     |      |             |         |           |       |   |        |   |       |
|     |      |             |         |           |       |   |        |   |       |
|     |      |             |         |           |       |   |        |   |       |
|     |      |             |         |           |       |   |        |   |       |
|     |      |             |         |           |       |   |        |   |       |
|     |      |             |         |           |       |   |        |   |       |
|     |      |             |         |           |       |   |        |   |       |
|     |      |             |         |           |       |   |        |   |       |
|     |      |             |         |           |       |   |        |   |       |
|     |      |             |         |           |       |   |        |   |       |
|     |      |             |         |           |       |   |        |   |       |
|     |      |             |         |           |       |   |        |   |       |
|     |      |             |         |           |       |   |        |   |       |
|     |      |             |         |           |       |   |        |   |       |
|     |      |             |         |           |       |   |        |   |       |
|     |      |             |         |           |       |   |        |   |       |

# ACCOUNTING LEDGER

PAGE.No.

Account Name And Number :

Year : _____        Month : _____

| No. | Date | Description | Account | Reference | Debit | — | Credit | + | Total |
|-----|------|-------------|---------|-----------|-------|---|--------|---|-------|
|     |      |             |         |           |       |   |        |   |       |
|     |      |             |         |           |       |   |        |   |       |
|     |      |             |         |           |       |   |        |   |       |
|     |      |             |         |           |       |   |        |   |       |
|     |      |             |         |           |       |   |        |   |       |
|     |      |             |         |           |       |   |        |   |       |
|     |      |             |         |           |       |   |        |   |       |
|     |      |             |         |           |       |   |        |   |       |
|     |      |             |         |           |       |   |        |   |       |
|     |      |             |         |           |       |   |        |   |       |
|     |      |             |         |           |       |   |        |   |       |
|     |      |             |         |           |       |   |        |   |       |
|     |      |             |         |           |       |   |        |   |       |
|     |      |             |         |           |       |   |        |   |       |
|     |      |             |         |           |       |   |        |   |       |
|     |      |             |         |           |       |   |        |   |       |
|     |      |             |         |           |       |   |        |   |       |
|     |      |             |         |           |       |   |        |   |       |
|     |      |             |         |           |       |   |        |   |       |
|     |      |             |         |           |       |   |        |   |       |
|     |      |             |         |           |       |   |        |   |       |
|     |      |             |         |           |       |   |        |   |       |
|     |      |             |         |           |       |   |        |   |       |
|     |      |             |         |           |       |   |        |   |       |
|     |      |             |         |           |       |   |        |   |       |
|     |      |             |         |           |       |   |        |   |       |
|     |      |             |         |           |       |   |        |   |       |
|     |      |             |         |           |       |   |        |   |       |

# ACCOUNTING LEDGER

**PAGE.No.**

**Account Name And Number :**

**Year : _____**                                          **Month : _____**

| No. | Date | Description | Account | Reference | Debit | − | Credit | + | Total |
|-----|------|-------------|---------|-----------|-------|---|--------|---|-------|
|     |      |             |         |           |       |   |        |   |       |
|     |      |             |         |           |       |   |        |   |       |
|     |      |             |         |           |       |   |        |   |       |
|     |      |             |         |           |       |   |        |   |       |
|     |      |             |         |           |       |   |        |   |       |
|     |      |             |         |           |       |   |        |   |       |
|     |      |             |         |           |       |   |        |   |       |
|     |      |             |         |           |       |   |        |   |       |
|     |      |             |         |           |       |   |        |   |       |
|     |      |             |         |           |       |   |        |   |       |
|     |      |             |         |           |       |   |        |   |       |
|     |      |             |         |           |       |   |        |   |       |
|     |      |             |         |           |       |   |        |   |       |
|     |      |             |         |           |       |   |        |   |       |
|     |      |             |         |           |       |   |        |   |       |
|     |      |             |         |           |       |   |        |   |       |
|     |      |             |         |           |       |   |        |   |       |
|     |      |             |         |           |       |   |        |   |       |
|     |      |             |         |           |       |   |        |   |       |
|     |      |             |         |           |       |   |        |   |       |
|     |      |             |         |           |       |   |        |   |       |
|     |      |             |         |           |       |   |        |   |       |
|     |      |             |         |           |       |   |        |   |       |
|     |      |             |         |           |       |   |        |   |       |
|     |      |             |         |           |       |   |        |   |       |
|     |      |             |         |           |       |   |        |   |       |
|     |      |             |         |           |       |   |        |   |       |
|     |      |             |         |           |       |   |        |   |       |

# ACCOUNTING LEDGER

**PAGE.No.**

**Account Name And Number :**

**Year : _____**                                    **Month : _____**

| No. | Date | Description | Account | Reference | Debit | − | Credit | + | Total |
|-----|------|-------------|---------|-----------|-------|---|--------|---|-------|
|     |      |             |         |           |       |   |        |   |       |
|     |      |             |         |           |       |   |        |   |       |
|     |      |             |         |           |       |   |        |   |       |
|     |      |             |         |           |       |   |        |   |       |
|     |      |             |         |           |       |   |        |   |       |
|     |      |             |         |           |       |   |        |   |       |
|     |      |             |         |           |       |   |        |   |       |
|     |      |             |         |           |       |   |        |   |       |
|     |      |             |         |           |       |   |        |   |       |
|     |      |             |         |           |       |   |        |   |       |
|     |      |             |         |           |       |   |        |   |       |
|     |      |             |         |           |       |   |        |   |       |
|     |      |             |         |           |       |   |        |   |       |
|     |      |             |         |           |       |   |        |   |       |
|     |      |             |         |           |       |   |        |   |       |
|     |      |             |         |           |       |   |        |   |       |
|     |      |             |         |           |       |   |        |   |       |
|     |      |             |         |           |       |   |        |   |       |
|     |      |             |         |           |       |   |        |   |       |
|     |      |             |         |           |       |   |        |   |       |
|     |      |             |         |           |       |   |        |   |       |
|     |      |             |         |           |       |   |        |   |       |
|     |      |             |         |           |       |   |        |   |       |
|     |      |             |         |           |       |   |        |   |       |
|     |      |             |         |           |       |   |        |   |       |
|     |      |             |         |           |       |   |        |   |       |

# ACCOUNTING LEDGER

PAGE.No.

**Account Name And Number :**

Year : _____                                     Month : _____

| No. | Date | Description | Account | Reference | Debit | − | Credit | + | Total |
|-----|------|-------------|---------|-----------|-------|---|--------|---|-------|
|     |      |             |         |           |       |   |        |   |       |
|     |      |             |         |           |       |   |        |   |       |
|     |      |             |         |           |       |   |        |   |       |
|     |      |             |         |           |       |   |        |   |       |
|     |      |             |         |           |       |   |        |   |       |
|     |      |             |         |           |       |   |        |   |       |
|     |      |             |         |           |       |   |        |   |       |
|     |      |             |         |           |       |   |        |   |       |
|     |      |             |         |           |       |   |        |   |       |
|     |      |             |         |           |       |   |        |   |       |
|     |      |             |         |           |       |   |        |   |       |
|     |      |             |         |           |       |   |        |   |       |
|     |      |             |         |           |       |   |        |   |       |
|     |      |             |         |           |       |   |        |   |       |
|     |      |             |         |           |       |   |        |   |       |
|     |      |             |         |           |       |   |        |   |       |
|     |      |             |         |           |       |   |        |   |       |
|     |      |             |         |           |       |   |        |   |       |
|     |      |             |         |           |       |   |        |   |       |
|     |      |             |         |           |       |   |        |   |       |
|     |      |             |         |           |       |   |        |   |       |
|     |      |             |         |           |       |   |        |   |       |
|     |      |             |         |           |       |   |        |   |       |
|     |      |             |         |           |       |   |        |   |       |
|     |      |             |         |           |       |   |        |   |       |
|     |      |             |         |           |       |   |        |   |       |

# ACCOUNTING LEDGER

**PAGE.No.**

**Account Name And Number :**

**Year : _____**                                                      **Month : _____**

| No. | Date | Description | Account | Reference | Debit | − | Credit | + | Total |
|-----|------|-------------|---------|-----------|-------|---|--------|---|-------|
|     |      |             |         |           |       |   |        |   |       |
|     |      |             |         |           |       |   |        |   |       |
|     |      |             |         |           |       |   |        |   |       |
|     |      |             |         |           |       |   |        |   |       |
|     |      |             |         |           |       |   |        |   |       |
|     |      |             |         |           |       |   |        |   |       |
|     |      |             |         |           |       |   |        |   |       |
|     |      |             |         |           |       |   |        |   |       |
|     |      |             |         |           |       |   |        |   |       |
|     |      |             |         |           |       |   |        |   |       |
|     |      |             |         |           |       |   |        |   |       |
|     |      |             |         |           |       |   |        |   |       |
|     |      |             |         |           |       |   |        |   |       |
|     |      |             |         |           |       |   |        |   |       |
|     |      |             |         |           |       |   |        |   |       |
|     |      |             |         |           |       |   |        |   |       |
|     |      |             |         |           |       |   |        |   |       |
|     |      |             |         |           |       |   |        |   |       |
|     |      |             |         |           |       |   |        |   |       |
|     |      |             |         |           |       |   |        |   |       |
|     |      |             |         |           |       |   |        |   |       |
|     |      |             |         |           |       |   |        |   |       |
|     |      |             |         |           |       |   |        |   |       |
|     |      |             |         |           |       |   |        |   |       |
|     |      |             |         |           |       |   |        |   |       |
|     |      |             |         |           |       |   |        |   |       |
|     |      |             |         |           |       |   |        |   |       |

# ACCOUNTING LEDGER

**PAGE.No.**

**Account Name And Number :**

**Year :** _____                                          **Month :** _____

| No. | Date | Description | Account | Reference | Debit | − | Credit | + | Total |
|-----|------|-------------|---------|-----------|-------|---|--------|---|-------|
|     |      |             |         |           |       |   |        |   |       |
|     |      |             |         |           |       |   |        |   |       |
|     |      |             |         |           |       |   |        |   |       |
|     |      |             |         |           |       |   |        |   |       |
|     |      |             |         |           |       |   |        |   |       |
|     |      |             |         |           |       |   |        |   |       |
|     |      |             |         |           |       |   |        |   |       |
|     |      |             |         |           |       |   |        |   |       |
|     |      |             |         |           |       |   |        |   |       |
|     |      |             |         |           |       |   |        |   |       |
|     |      |             |         |           |       |   |        |   |       |
|     |      |             |         |           |       |   |        |   |       |
|     |      |             |         |           |       |   |        |   |       |
|     |      |             |         |           |       |   |        |   |       |
|     |      |             |         |           |       |   |        |   |       |
|     |      |             |         |           |       |   |        |   |       |
|     |      |             |         |           |       |   |        |   |       |
|     |      |             |         |           |       |   |        |   |       |
|     |      |             |         |           |       |   |        |   |       |
|     |      |             |         |           |       |   |        |   |       |
|     |      |             |         |           |       |   |        |   |       |
|     |      |             |         |           |       |   |        |   |       |
|     |      |             |         |           |       |   |        |   |       |
|     |      |             |         |           |       |   |        |   |       |
|     |      |             |         |           |       |   |        |   |       |
|     |      |             |         |           |       |   |        |   |       |
|     |      |             |         |           |       |   |        |   |       |

# ACCOUNTING LEDGER

**PAGE.No.**

**Account Name And Number :**

**Year : _____**                                    **Month : _____**

| No. | Date | Description | Account | Reference | Debit | − | Credit | + | Total |
|-----|------|-------------|---------|-----------|-------|---|--------|---|-------|
|     |      |             |         |           |       |   |        |   |       |
|     |      |             |         |           |       |   |        |   |       |
|     |      |             |         |           |       |   |        |   |       |
|     |      |             |         |           |       |   |        |   |       |
|     |      |             |         |           |       |   |        |   |       |
|     |      |             |         |           |       |   |        |   |       |
|     |      |             |         |           |       |   |        |   |       |
|     |      |             |         |           |       |   |        |   |       |
|     |      |             |         |           |       |   |        |   |       |
|     |      |             |         |           |       |   |        |   |       |
|     |      |             |         |           |       |   |        |   |       |
|     |      |             |         |           |       |   |        |   |       |
|     |      |             |         |           |       |   |        |   |       |
|     |      |             |         |           |       |   |        |   |       |
|     |      |             |         |           |       |   |        |   |       |
|     |      |             |         |           |       |   |        |   |       |
|     |      |             |         |           |       |   |        |   |       |
|     |      |             |         |           |       |   |        |   |       |
|     |      |             |         |           |       |   |        |   |       |
|     |      |             |         |           |       |   |        |   |       |
|     |      |             |         |           |       |   |        |   |       |
|     |      |             |         |           |       |   |        |   |       |
|     |      |             |         |           |       |   |        |   |       |
|     |      |             |         |           |       |   |        |   |       |
|     |      |             |         |           |       |   |        |   |       |
|     |      |             |         |           |       |   |        |   |       |

# ACCOUNTING LEDGER

PAGE.No.

Account Name And Number :

Year : _____                                                Month : _____

| No. | Date | Description | Account | Reference | Debit | — | Credit | + | Total |
|-----|------|-------------|---------|-----------|-------|---|--------|---|-------|
| | | | | | | | | | |
| | | | | | | | | | |
| | | | | | | | | | |
| | | | | | | | | | |
| | | | | | | | | | |
| | | | | | | | | | |
| | | | | | | | | | |
| | | | | | | | | | |
| | | | | | | | | | |
| | | | | | | | | | |
| | | | | | | | | | |
| | | | | | | | | | |
| | | | | | | | | | |
| | | | | | | | | | |
| | | | | | | | | | |
| | | | | | | | | | |
| | | | | | | | | | |
| | | | | | | | | | |
| | | | | | | | | | |
| | | | | | | | | | |
| | | | | | | | | | |
| | | | | | | | | | |
| | | | | | | | | | |
| | | | | | | | | | |
| | | | | | | | | | |
| | | | | | | | | | |

# ACCOUNTING LEDGER

**PAGE.No.**

**Account Name And Number :**

**Year : _____**　　　　　　　　　　　　　　　**Month : _____**

| No. | Date | Description | Account | Reference | Debit | − | Credit | + | Total |
|-----|------|-------------|---------|-----------|-------|---|--------|---|-------|
|  |  |  |  |  |  |  |  |  |  |
|  |  |  |  |  |  |  |  |  |  |
|  |  |  |  |  |  |  |  |  |  |
|  |  |  |  |  |  |  |  |  |  |
|  |  |  |  |  |  |  |  |  |  |
|  |  |  |  |  |  |  |  |  |  |
|  |  |  |  |  |  |  |  |  |  |
|  |  |  |  |  |  |  |  |  |  |
|  |  |  |  |  |  |  |  |  |  |
|  |  |  |  |  |  |  |  |  |  |
|  |  |  |  |  |  |  |  |  |  |
|  |  |  |  |  |  |  |  |  |  |
|  |  |  |  |  |  |  |  |  |  |
|  |  |  |  |  |  |  |  |  |  |
|  |  |  |  |  |  |  |  |  |  |
|  |  |  |  |  |  |  |  |  |  |
|  |  |  |  |  |  |  |  |  |  |
|  |  |  |  |  |  |  |  |  |  |
|  |  |  |  |  |  |  |  |  |  |
|  |  |  |  |  |  |  |  |  |  |
|  |  |  |  |  |  |  |  |  |  |
|  |  |  |  |  |  |  |  |  |  |
|  |  |  |  |  |  |  |  |  |  |
|  |  |  |  |  |  |  |  |  |  |
|  |  |  |  |  |  |  |  |  |  |
|  |  |  |  |  |  |  |  |  |  |
|  |  |  |  |  |  |  |  |  |  |
|  |  |  |  |  |  |  |  |  |  |
|  |  |  |  |  |  |  |  |  |  |
|  |  |  |  |  |  |  |  |  |  |

# ACCOUNTING LEDGER

PAGE.No.

Account Name And Number :

Year : _____                                      Month : _____

| No. | Date | Description | Account | Reference | Debit | − | Credit | + | Total |
|-----|------|-------------|---------|-----------|-------|---|--------|---|-------|
|     |      |             |         |           |       |   |        |   |       |
|     |      |             |         |           |       |   |        |   |       |
|     |      |             |         |           |       |   |        |   |       |
|     |      |             |         |           |       |   |        |   |       |
|     |      |             |         |           |       |   |        |   |       |
|     |      |             |         |           |       |   |        |   |       |
|     |      |             |         |           |       |   |        |   |       |
|     |      |             |         |           |       |   |        |   |       |
|     |      |             |         |           |       |   |        |   |       |
|     |      |             |         |           |       |   |        |   |       |
|     |      |             |         |           |       |   |        |   |       |
|     |      |             |         |           |       |   |        |   |       |
|     |      |             |         |           |       |   |        |   |       |
|     |      |             |         |           |       |   |        |   |       |
|     |      |             |         |           |       |   |        |   |       |
|     |      |             |         |           |       |   |        |   |       |
|     |      |             |         |           |       |   |        |   |       |
|     |      |             |         |           |       |   |        |   |       |
|     |      |             |         |           |       |   |        |   |       |
|     |      |             |         |           |       |   |        |   |       |
|     |      |             |         |           |       |   |        |   |       |
|     |      |             |         |           |       |   |        |   |       |
|     |      |             |         |           |       |   |        |   |       |
|     |      |             |         |           |       |   |        |   |       |
|     |      |             |         |           |       |   |        |   |       |
|     |      |             |         |           |       |   |        |   |       |
|     |      |             |         |           |       |   |        |   |       |
|     |      |             |         |           |       |   |        |   |       |

# ACCOUNTING LEDGER

**PAGE.No.**

**Account Name And Number :**

**Year : _____**              **Month : _____**

| No. | Date | Description | Account | Reference | Debit | − | Credit | + | Total |
|-----|------|-------------|---------|-----------|-------|---|--------|---|-------|
|     |      |             |         |           |       |   |        |   |       |
|     |      |             |         |           |       |   |        |   |       |
|     |      |             |         |           |       |   |        |   |       |
|     |      |             |         |           |       |   |        |   |       |
|     |      |             |         |           |       |   |        |   |       |
|     |      |             |         |           |       |   |        |   |       |
|     |      |             |         |           |       |   |        |   |       |
|     |      |             |         |           |       |   |        |   |       |
|     |      |             |         |           |       |   |        |   |       |
|     |      |             |         |           |       |   |        |   |       |
|     |      |             |         |           |       |   |        |   |       |
|     |      |             |         |           |       |   |        |   |       |
|     |      |             |         |           |       |   |        |   |       |
|     |      |             |         |           |       |   |        |   |       |
|     |      |             |         |           |       |   |        |   |       |
|     |      |             |         |           |       |   |        |   |       |
|     |      |             |         |           |       |   |        |   |       |
|     |      |             |         |           |       |   |        |   |       |
|     |      |             |         |           |       |   |        |   |       |
|     |      |             |         |           |       |   |        |   |       |
|     |      |             |         |           |       |   |        |   |       |
|     |      |             |         |           |       |   |        |   |       |
|     |      |             |         |           |       |   |        |   |       |
|     |      |             |         |           |       |   |        |   |       |
|     |      |             |         |           |       |   |        |   |       |
|     |      |             |         |           |       |   |        |   |       |

# ACCOUNTING LEDGER

PAGE.No.

Account Name And Number :

Year : _____                                             Month : _____

| No. | Date | Description | Account | Reference | Debit | − | Credit | + | Total |
|-----|------|-------------|---------|-----------|-------|---|--------|---|-------|
|     |      |             |         |           |       |   |        |   |       |
|     |      |             |         |           |       |   |        |   |       |
|     |      |             |         |           |       |   |        |   |       |
|     |      |             |         |           |       |   |        |   |       |
|     |      |             |         |           |       |   |        |   |       |
|     |      |             |         |           |       |   |        |   |       |
|     |      |             |         |           |       |   |        |   |       |
|     |      |             |         |           |       |   |        |   |       |
|     |      |             |         |           |       |   |        |   |       |
|     |      |             |         |           |       |   |        |   |       |
|     |      |             |         |           |       |   |        |   |       |
|     |      |             |         |           |       |   |        |   |       |
|     |      |             |         |           |       |   |        |   |       |
|     |      |             |         |           |       |   |        |   |       |
|     |      |             |         |           |       |   |        |   |       |
|     |      |             |         |           |       |   |        |   |       |
|     |      |             |         |           |       |   |        |   |       |
|     |      |             |         |           |       |   |        |   |       |
|     |      |             |         |           |       |   |        |   |       |
|     |      |             |         |           |       |   |        |   |       |
|     |      |             |         |           |       |   |        |   |       |
|     |      |             |         |           |       |   |        |   |       |
|     |      |             |         |           |       |   |        |   |       |
|     |      |             |         |           |       |   |        |   |       |
|     |      |             |         |           |       |   |        |   |       |

# ACCOUNTING LEDGER

**PAGE.No.**

**Account Name And Number :**

**Year :** _____

**Month :** _____

| No. | Date | Description | Account | Reference | Debit | — | Credit | + | Total |
|-----|------|-------------|---------|-----------|-------|---|--------|---|-------|
|     |      |             |         |           |       |   |        |   |       |
|     |      |             |         |           |       |   |        |   |       |
|     |      |             |         |           |       |   |        |   |       |
|     |      |             |         |           |       |   |        |   |       |
|     |      |             |         |           |       |   |        |   |       |
|     |      |             |         |           |       |   |        |   |       |
|     |      |             |         |           |       |   |        |   |       |
|     |      |             |         |           |       |   |        |   |       |
|     |      |             |         |           |       |   |        |   |       |
|     |      |             |         |           |       |   |        |   |       |
|     |      |             |         |           |       |   |        |   |       |
|     |      |             |         |           |       |   |        |   |       |
|     |      |             |         |           |       |   |        |   |       |
|     |      |             |         |           |       |   |        |   |       |
|     |      |             |         |           |       |   |        |   |       |
|     |      |             |         |           |       |   |        |   |       |
|     |      |             |         |           |       |   |        |   |       |
|     |      |             |         |           |       |   |        |   |       |
|     |      |             |         |           |       |   |        |   |       |
|     |      |             |         |           |       |   |        |   |       |
|     |      |             |         |           |       |   |        |   |       |
|     |      |             |         |           |       |   |        |   |       |
|     |      |             |         |           |       |   |        |   |       |
|     |      |             |         |           |       |   |        |   |       |
|     |      |             |         |           |       |   |        |   |       |
|     |      |             |         |           |       |   |        |   |       |
|     |      |             |         |           |       |   |        |   |       |
|     |      |             |         |           |       |   |        |   |       |

# ACCOUNTING LEDGER

**PAGE.No.**

**Account Name And Number :**

**Year : _____**                                          **Month : _____**

| No. | Date | Description | Account | Reference | Debit | − | Credit | + | Total |
|-----|------|-------------|---------|-----------|-------|---|--------|---|-------|
|     |      |             |         |           |       |   |        |   |       |
|     |      |             |         |           |       |   |        |   |       |
|     |      |             |         |           |       |   |        |   |       |
|     |      |             |         |           |       |   |        |   |       |
|     |      |             |         |           |       |   |        |   |       |
|     |      |             |         |           |       |   |        |   |       |
|     |      |             |         |           |       |   |        |   |       |
|     |      |             |         |           |       |   |        |   |       |
|     |      |             |         |           |       |   |        |   |       |
|     |      |             |         |           |       |   |        |   |       |
|     |      |             |         |           |       |   |        |   |       |
|     |      |             |         |           |       |   |        |   |       |
|     |      |             |         |           |       |   |        |   |       |
|     |      |             |         |           |       |   |        |   |       |
|     |      |             |         |           |       |   |        |   |       |
|     |      |             |         |           |       |   |        |   |       |
|     |      |             |         |           |       |   |        |   |       |
|     |      |             |         |           |       |   |        |   |       |
|     |      |             |         |           |       |   |        |   |       |
|     |      |             |         |           |       |   |        |   |       |
|     |      |             |         |           |       |   |        |   |       |
|     |      |             |         |           |       |   |        |   |       |
|     |      |             |         |           |       |   |        |   |       |
|     |      |             |         |           |       |   |        |   |       |
|     |      |             |         |           |       |   |        |   |       |
|     |      |             |         |           |       |   |        |   |       |
|     |      |             |         |           |       |   |        |   |       |
|     |      |             |         |           |       |   |        |   |       |

# ACCOUNTING LEDGER

**PAGE.No.**

**Account Name And Number :**

**Year :** _____

**Month :** _____

| No. | Date | Description | Account | Reference | Debit | − | Credit | + | Total |
|-----|------|-------------|---------|-----------|-------|---|--------|---|-------|
|     |      |             |         |           |       |   |        |   |       |
|     |      |             |         |           |       |   |        |   |       |
|     |      |             |         |           |       |   |        |   |       |
|     |      |             |         |           |       |   |        |   |       |
|     |      |             |         |           |       |   |        |   |       |
|     |      |             |         |           |       |   |        |   |       |
|     |      |             |         |           |       |   |        |   |       |
|     |      |             |         |           |       |   |        |   |       |
|     |      |             |         |           |       |   |        |   |       |
|     |      |             |         |           |       |   |        |   |       |
|     |      |             |         |           |       |   |        |   |       |
|     |      |             |         |           |       |   |        |   |       |
|     |      |             |         |           |       |   |        |   |       |
|     |      |             |         |           |       |   |        |   |       |
|     |      |             |         |           |       |   |        |   |       |
|     |      |             |         |           |       |   |        |   |       |
|     |      |             |         |           |       |   |        |   |       |
|     |      |             |         |           |       |   |        |   |       |
|     |      |             |         |           |       |   |        |   |       |
|     |      |             |         |           |       |   |        |   |       |
|     |      |             |         |           |       |   |        |   |       |
|     |      |             |         |           |       |   |        |   |       |
|     |      |             |         |           |       |   |        |   |       |
|     |      |             |         |           |       |   |        |   |       |
|     |      |             |         |           |       |   |        |   |       |
|     |      |             |         |           |       |   |        |   |       |
|     |      |             |         |           |       |   |        |   |       |

# ACCOUNTING LEDGER

PAGE.No.

**Account Name And Number :**

Year : _____          Month : _____

| No. | Date | Description | Account | Reference | Debit | − | Credit | + | Total |
|-----|------|-------------|---------|-----------|-------|---|--------|---|-------|
|     |      |             |         |           |       |   |        |   |       |
|     |      |             |         |           |       |   |        |   |       |
|     |      |             |         |           |       |   |        |   |       |
|     |      |             |         |           |       |   |        |   |       |
|     |      |             |         |           |       |   |        |   |       |
|     |      |             |         |           |       |   |        |   |       |
|     |      |             |         |           |       |   |        |   |       |
|     |      |             |         |           |       |   |        |   |       |
|     |      |             |         |           |       |   |        |   |       |
|     |      |             |         |           |       |   |        |   |       |
|     |      |             |         |           |       |   |        |   |       |
|     |      |             |         |           |       |   |        |   |       |
|     |      |             |         |           |       |   |        |   |       |
|     |      |             |         |           |       |   |        |   |       |
|     |      |             |         |           |       |   |        |   |       |
|     |      |             |         |           |       |   |        |   |       |
|     |      |             |         |           |       |   |        |   |       |
|     |      |             |         |           |       |   |        |   |       |
|     |      |             |         |           |       |   |        |   |       |
|     |      |             |         |           |       |   |        |   |       |
|     |      |             |         |           |       |   |        |   |       |
|     |      |             |         |           |       |   |        |   |       |
|     |      |             |         |           |       |   |        |   |       |
|     |      |             |         |           |       |   |        |   |       |
|     |      |             |         |           |       |   |        |   |       |

# ACCOUNTING LEDGER

**PAGE.No.**

**Account Name And Number :**

**Year : _____**                                   **Month : _____**

| No. | Date | Description | Account | Reference | Debit | − | Credit | + | Total |
|-----|------|-------------|---------|-----------|-------|---|--------|---|-------|
|     |      |             |         |           |       |   |        |   |       |
|     |      |             |         |           |       |   |        |   |       |
|     |      |             |         |           |       |   |        |   |       |
|     |      |             |         |           |       |   |        |   |       |
|     |      |             |         |           |       |   |        |   |       |
|     |      |             |         |           |       |   |        |   |       |
|     |      |             |         |           |       |   |        |   |       |
|     |      |             |         |           |       |   |        |   |       |
|     |      |             |         |           |       |   |        |   |       |
|     |      |             |         |           |       |   |        |   |       |
|     |      |             |         |           |       |   |        |   |       |
|     |      |             |         |           |       |   |        |   |       |
|     |      |             |         |           |       |   |        |   |       |
|     |      |             |         |           |       |   |        |   |       |
|     |      |             |         |           |       |   |        |   |       |
|     |      |             |         |           |       |   |        |   |       |
|     |      |             |         |           |       |   |        |   |       |
|     |      |             |         |           |       |   |        |   |       |
|     |      |             |         |           |       |   |        |   |       |
|     |      |             |         |           |       |   |        |   |       |
|     |      |             |         |           |       |   |        |   |       |
|     |      |             |         |           |       |   |        |   |       |
|     |      |             |         |           |       |   |        |   |       |
|     |      |             |         |           |       |   |        |   |       |
|     |      |             |         |           |       |   |        |   |       |
|     |      |             |         |           |       |   |        |   |       |
|     |      |             |         |           |       |   |        |   |       |
|     |      |             |         |           |       |   |        |   |       |
|     |      |             |         |           |       |   |        |   |       |
|     |      |             |         |           |       |   |        |   |       |

# ACCOUNTING LEDGER

PAGE.No.

**Account Name And Number :**

Year : _____                                                    Month : _____

| No. | Date | Description | Account | Reference | Debit | − | Credit | + | Total |
|-----|------|-------------|---------|-----------|-------|---|--------|---|-------|
|     |      |             |         |           |       |   |        |   |       |
|     |      |             |         |           |       |   |        |   |       |
|     |      |             |         |           |       |   |        |   |       |
|     |      |             |         |           |       |   |        |   |       |
|     |      |             |         |           |       |   |        |   |       |
|     |      |             |         |           |       |   |        |   |       |
|     |      |             |         |           |       |   |        |   |       |
|     |      |             |         |           |       |   |        |   |       |
|     |      |             |         |           |       |   |        |   |       |
|     |      |             |         |           |       |   |        |   |       |
|     |      |             |         |           |       |   |        |   |       |
|     |      |             |         |           |       |   |        |   |       |
|     |      |             |         |           |       |   |        |   |       |
|     |      |             |         |           |       |   |        |   |       |
|     |      |             |         |           |       |   |        |   |       |
|     |      |             |         |           |       |   |        |   |       |
|     |      |             |         |           |       |   |        |   |       |
|     |      |             |         |           |       |   |        |   |       |
|     |      |             |         |           |       |   |        |   |       |
|     |      |             |         |           |       |   |        |   |       |
|     |      |             |         |           |       |   |        |   |       |
|     |      |             |         |           |       |   |        |   |       |
|     |      |             |         |           |       |   |        |   |       |
|     |      |             |         |           |       |   |        |   |       |
|     |      |             |         |           |       |   |        |   |       |
|     |      |             |         |           |       |   |        |   |       |
|     |      |             |         |           |       |   |        |   |       |
|     |      |             |         |           |       |   |        |   |       |

# ACCOUNTING LEDGER

PAGE.No.

**Account Name And Number :**

**Year : _____**　　　　　　　　　　　　　　**Month : _____**

| No. | Date | Description | Account | Reference | Debit | − | Credit | + | Total |
|-----|------|-------------|---------|-----------|-------|---|--------|---|-------|
|     |      |             |         |           |       |   |        |   |       |
|     |      |             |         |           |       |   |        |   |       |
|     |      |             |         |           |       |   |        |   |       |
|     |      |             |         |           |       |   |        |   |       |
|     |      |             |         |           |       |   |        |   |       |
|     |      |             |         |           |       |   |        |   |       |
|     |      |             |         |           |       |   |        |   |       |
|     |      |             |         |           |       |   |        |   |       |
|     |      |             |         |           |       |   |        |   |       |
|     |      |             |         |           |       |   |        |   |       |
|     |      |             |         |           |       |   |        |   |       |
|     |      |             |         |           |       |   |        |   |       |
|     |      |             |         |           |       |   |        |   |       |
|     |      |             |         |           |       |   |        |   |       |
|     |      |             |         |           |       |   |        |   |       |
|     |      |             |         |           |       |   |        |   |       |
|     |      |             |         |           |       |   |        |   |       |
|     |      |             |         |           |       |   |        |   |       |
|     |      |             |         |           |       |   |        |   |       |
|     |      |             |         |           |       |   |        |   |       |
|     |      |             |         |           |       |   |        |   |       |
|     |      |             |         |           |       |   |        |   |       |
|     |      |             |         |           |       |   |        |   |       |
|     |      |             |         |           |       |   |        |   |       |
|     |      |             |         |           |       |   |        |   |       |

# Thank you!

WE ARE GLAD THAT YOU PURCHASED OUR BOOK!
PLEASE LET US KNOW HOW WE CAN IMPROVE IT!
YOUR FEEDBACK IS ESSENTIAL TO US.

Contact us at:

M log'Sin@gmail.com

---

JUST TITLE THE EMAIL 'CREATIVE' AND WE WILL

GIVE YOU SOME EXTRA SURPRISES!

www.ingramcontent.com/pod-product-compliance
Lightning Source LLC
Chambersburg PA
CBHW081822200326

41597CB00023B/4352